MARRIAGE

MARRIAGE
AN INTERFAITH GUIDE
FOR ALL COUPLES

Edited by

REV. RABAN HATHORN, O.S.B.
REV. WILLIAM H. GENNÉ
RABBI MORDECAI L. BRILL

ASSOCIATION PRESS · NEW YORK
ABBEY PRESS · ST. MEINRAD, INDIANA

Introduction

This book is unique.

Most writers on marriage, in the effort to reach as wide an audience as possible, have tended to clothe their values and ideals in very general terms without specific religious references.

Our contributors were asked to articulate as clearly and as fully as possible all of the richness of the Judeo-Christian heritage as it relates to that great venture of faith we know as marriage.

In an ecumenical age when Catholic, Jew, and Protestant are realizing how close we are in God's family, it seemed wise to the editors to provide couples with a statement that sets forth clearly, without apology or equivocation, the richness of God's wisdom and love concerning marriage.

This book is *not* directed to those who unite two different faiths in a religiously mixed marriage. Rather it is a compendium of insights from our three traditions which we believe will enrich any couple. Each of our treasuries of faith has its own unique contribution to make. By bringing them together in one volume, we hope to make them more readily available.

We have not tried to gloss over our differences. They have been frankly recognized and set forth at appropriate points. These as yet unresolved differences in our understandings are a challenge to continued growth. Different couples, even in the same congregation, will find variations in the understandings of their religious heritage. We hope this volume will help to illuminate their faith and suggest a model for the discussion of these basic affirmations about life.

Marriage is a venture of faith. When two persons make a commitment to unite their lives in fidelity and love so long as they both shall live, they are starting a new stream of history—a new dynasty, if you please. They will need all of the resources available to sustain them in that commitment, to nourish their idealism and love, and to help them attain the fullness God intended for their marriage. We believe our God offers resources sufficient to any difficulty a couple may encounter.

Marriage may be thought of in three ways:

As *Vocation:* God, Our Father-Creator, has a purpose, an intention, a destiny for our lives. Jews feel that it is the intention of God that everyone should marry. Protestants and Catholics give equal sanctity to the single or married state. All three agree, however, that a person's decision to marry or not to marry should be a response to his understanding of God's call, or vocation, for his life. Such a response becomes part of a person's total religious commitment and calls forth his highest, deepest, and most sustained effort.

As *Covenant:* Marriage is more than a contract between two persons. It is interesting to note that in civil law, marriage is the one contract that cannot be dissolved by the mutual consent of the two contracting parties. The interests of the whole society in the success of the marriage are too vital to allow it to be dissolved at will.

Religiously, marriage is regarded by all three faiths as a covenant which involves not only the partners and the community in which they live but also the Father-God in whom we live and move and have our being. This covenant involves a four-way compact between a man, a woman, their community of faith, and their God. Each acknowledges that the undertaking of marriage involves an interlocking set of responsibilities and claims upon each other. In modern organizational jargon we would call this a "mutual support system."

In this covenant, God not only sets the norms and standards for behavior, He also promises to help the couple achieve their fullest potentiality. The couple, acknowledging that their love is a gift from God, pledge their fullest devotion to the fulfillment of their vows. The community of faith (and the state that also recognizes the marriage) pledges its support to the couple. Thus, each helping the other, the marriage is built, aided, and protected by this covenant of mutual concern and love.

As *Sacrament:* At the heart of every marriage is a mystery. How can so great a love enter into the experience of mere mortals? Who plants the love for each other in the hearts of a man and a woman? Many men and women have found in their love for each other the increased awareness of the love of God in their lives.

The classic definition of a sacrament is "the outward and visible sign of an inner, spiritual reality." The wedding and continuing marriage of a loving couple is for some of our communions just such a sacrament. In fact, it is the one sacrament that the couple confer upon each other. The officiating priest or clergyman simply witnesses the ceremony—the couple marry each other. The other communions who may not regard marriage as a sacrament in the technical sense do acknowledge that a true marriage has a sacramental character about it.

At the heart of this sacramental concept is the acknowledgment that the love, strength, forgiveness, and joy of God are transmitted to each through the other partner in marriage. No intermediary is necessary. This sacramental concept lifts the religious marriage far above the human level. This is why marriage at its best is the very vestibule of paradise.

And so we offer you this volume to help you realize in your marriage the fullness of marriage as an ongoing vocation, covenant, and sacrament.

As we have worked together, we have been acutely aware of the great stresses and strains that changes in our world have been forcing on marriage. New knowledge has brought great freedom to decide in many areas of life. Many of the issues are complex and difficult. Our social institutions often seem slow in their ability to adapt to changing situations. The age-old perversities of greed, selfishness, fear, and ignorance still plague our human relationships.

Notwithstanding, we affirm that God is laboring with all men and women of good will to build a better world. His love still inspires the hearts of men and women. He still entrusts babies, his most fragile creation, to fathers and mothers.

God loves us, even before we become what he wants us to be. He has given to the couples who read this book a great love as an evidence of his great love for us. In response to that love, may we pledge ourselves to strengthen and enrich our own marriage and to work for a society in which each person may enjoy fulfillment in dignity, justice, and peace.

Rev. Raban Hathorn, O.S.B.
Rev. William Genné
Rabbi Mordecai Brill

About the Editors

REVEREND RABAN HATHORN, a priest and monk of the Order of St. Benedict, is an editor of books on marriage and family published by Abbey Press, St. Meinrad, Indiana. He was for twenty years the editor of MARRIAGE MAGAZINE (formerly THE GRAIL) and is involved in Cana Conferences and Retreats for Married Couples.

REVEREND WILLIAM H. GENNÉ is Coordinator of Family Ministries for the National Council of the Churches of Christ in the United States and serves as Secretary for the Interfaith Commission on Marriage and Family Life created by the National Council, the Synagogue Council of America, and the United States Catholic Conference. He and his wife have written THE MINISTRY OF PARENTS, CHRISTIANS AND THE CRISIS IN SEX MORALITY, CAMPING WITH THE FAMILY. They have also co-authored the scripts of sound filmstrips entitled THE CHRISTIAN PARENTS' KIT.

RABBI MORDECAL L. BRILL, a full-time member of the staff of the American Foundation of Religion and Psychiatry, New York City, is also a member of the American Association of Marriage Counselors and the American Association of Pastoral Counselors and chairman of the Commission on Marriage and Family of the Synagogue Council of America. He is a founder and former chairman of the National Interfaith Commission on Marriage and Family Life. Rabbi Brill is married and the father of three children.

A Joint Statement on Marriage and Family Life in the United States

Keenly aware of the role religion ascribes to the home and family life and keenly aware of the powerful and pervasive social conditions which threaten to undermine human dignity, marriage and family life in America, we, as representatives of the major religions —Catholic, Jewish, Orthodox, and Protestant—wish to bring the religious teachings of our respective faiths to bear upon our society and to join with all men of good will to create a healthier social climate in which family life in America can flourish and be strong.

There are large areas of agreement and numerous possibilities for joint programs and action, although we recognize and respect the differences of approach, emphases and contributions of each major faith.

To help families develop foundations for personally meaningful and socially responsible behavior, we offer the following affirmations on which our historic faiths unite.

We believe, and unite in affirming, that God, the Creator of the Universe and the Father of all mankind, did create us male and female and did establish families as part of his Divine Plan. Because of our understanding of this plan, we believe and unite in affirming that our sexuality is a wondrous gift from God to be accepted with thanksgiving and used within marriage with reverence and joy.

We believe and unite in affirming that our understanding of God's plan for marriage ideally calls for lifelong commitment in fidelity to a continuing, supportive relationship in which each partner helps the other to develop to fullest capacity. We are united in our belief that God is an active partner in sustaining and enriching the husband-wife relationship in marriage.

We believe and unite in affirming that children are a trust from God and that parenthood is a joyous, though strenuous, adventure in partnership with God for the procreation and nurturing of each child. Parenthood calls for the responsible use of all of our God-given talents and abilities in this adventure.

We believe and unite in affirming that family life is the cradle of personality and character for each child and creates an environment for the societal values of each succeeding generation as well as the principal source of meaningful personal relations for each adult member of our society. All children need a father and a mother firmly united in love to guide their growth into manhood or womanhood and to provide the emotional security that fosters development toward mature and responsible relationships.

We believe that the family is the cornerstone of our society. It shapes the attitudes, the hopes, the ambitions, the values of every citizen. The child is usually damaged when family living collapses. When this happens on a massive scale, the community itself is crippled.

There are no easy answers to all the complex problems facing marriage and family living in the world today, and we are aware that there are many fronts on which we must work. We can never finish the task; neither are we free to ignore it.

Therefore, we the major religious groups in the U.S., join forces in exploring all ways and means available to preserve and strengthen family life in America to the end that each person may enjoy fulfillment in dignity, justice, and peace.

Approved for release June 8, 1966 by the
UNITED STATES CATHOLIC CONFERENCE
Family Life Bureau
NATIONAL COUNCIL OF THE CHURCHES OF CHRIST
in the U.S.A.
Commission on Marriage and Family
SYNAGOGUE COUNCIL OF AMERICA
Committee on the Family

Contents

PART I

•

WHAT YOU BRING
TO YOUR MARRIAGE

1

Your Manhood or Your Womanhood

•

CLAYTON AND MYRA BARBEAU

Clayton and Myra Barbeau, married eighteen years, have eight children and reside in a three-story Victorian house in San Francisco's Haight-Ashbury. Clayton is editor of *Way-Catholic Viewpoints*, an award-winning national magazine published by the Franciscan Fathers, author of *The Head of the Family*, now in its fourth printing and foreign editions, editor of *Art, Obscenity and Your Children*, and his articles have appeared in many national publications. Myra is his "best editor," commenting on, improving, and typing his materials. Together, they are in demand as lecturers on marriage and family life and are involved in neighborhood organizations, ecumenical and inter-racial projects, and teaching programs.

•

MAN'S CONFRONTATION WITH WOMAN has been with us since Adam first greeted Eve with that wondrous love song, "This is bone of my bones, flesh of my flesh; she shall be called woman because she was taken out of man." And the same man who sang that song of discovery and awe was later to seek to pin the rap for his fall from grace upon his wife: "The woman thou gavest to be with me, she gave me of the tree and I did eat."

Since the dawn of history, then, the relationship of the sexes has been one marked by love songs and vituperation, troubadour poetry and infidelity, the sweet taste of wedding cakes and the bitter ashes of mutual recriminations. Indeed, the man-woman relationship, its ardor, triumphs, comedies, failures, joys, tragedies and beauties are the substance of the major portion of the literature and art of the world for the simple reason that they are the basic stuff of daily life.

When the official witness of Church or Synagogue asks "Do you, ———, take this woman. . . . Do you, ———, take this man . . . to be your lawfully wedded spouse . . . ?" his words mean what they say. It is our very manliness, our very womanliness, that we bring to our marriage. It is by virtue of our being "man" and "woman" that we are able to marry at all. The officiant, however, has not said merely "man . . . woman," he has also called us by our name: this particular man, this particular woman. We are bringing to one another the total uniqueness of our personhood.

We meet here as equals, as persons. Our being joined in matrimony as man and wife does not mean for either of us that we now enter a relationship of unequals as persons. Those who have been deceived into thinking so have need to remind themselves of the thundering, revolutionary idea propounded in the first chapter of Genesis: "And God created mankind, male and female he created them." That truth was a radical departure from the prevailing notion of the day which held that women were little more than chattel. St. Paul was only underscoring that same fundamental affirmation of the equality-as-persons of male and female when he said that men must love their wives as their own flesh and blood. The concept of the fundamental equality of man and woman is basic to the whole Judeo-Christian view of mankind. Any notion of the manly "role" in marriage, of the womanly "role" in marriage, which attacks the personhood of the other, which denies to the other the respect and reverence and opportunity for development of intellectual, spiritual, artistic, or social capacities of the other, is foreign to the Judeo-Christian view of marriage.

Indeed, these two are being called by name to help one another in the lifelong task of growing to full maturity as persons. It is not good for man to be alone. They have felt the truth of that and so they join together to bring to one another all the goods that flow from two who have joined in the creation of a new entity, the "we" of marriage. From the moment of the vows, he now exists no longer only as this man, but as "her husband," she is now "his wife." They call forth from one another a new response, a response as "two in one flesh." Here there is no burying of personal identities, no loss of personhood, but an enrichment to each of them, the development in each of them of a new capacity for relating to one another and to the world at large.

When speaking on marriage not long ago, one of the writers commented that he felt "slightly fraudulent" because the other half of the marriage was not present to share the platform. He was corrected during the discussion period by a participant who said: "Myra was here, she was present in all that you said." It was a high compliment and passed on only because it offered an insight we think valid: that in a marriage, good or bad, one partner is always "present" in the attitudes, words, actions of the other. A husband's attitude toward other women reflects his attitude toward his wife; a woman's attitude toward men reflects her attitude toward her husband. Their attitudes toward marriage are a reflection of the marriage they have. How they relate to the one other person in the most intimate personal relationship on earth will determine to a large extent how they relate to every other person in the world.

Recently a young man, married only a few years, commented: "I used to have five guns: three rifles and two pistols. I sold them all recently. I haven't been interested in them since I got married. I needed them to prove I was manly, I guess, the great hunter, the ready man with the weapon, whatever. Anyway, she's made that sort of thing unnecessary. She's convinced me I'm a man. Not just in bed, either, because I was lousy at that, too, before she got me to see that it wasn't anything I did, it was who I was that counted."

What if, however, whenever she had said, "I love you," the little voice in his head had continued to respond, "But I'm unlovable. You're just saying that"? Not all the fears and stumbling blocks to full love of another person are so readily overcome as the young man's. A woman, happily married by most people's standards, mother of four, told us she had never deeply enjoyed sexual intercourse with her husband. A therapist finally broke through and discovered that when she was five years old she had come home and innocently asked her parents what a new word she had just heard meant. They had together washed her mouth out with soap and beaten her severely and sent her to bed without supper warning her never to use that word again. Because that word was a vulgarism for sexual intercourse, she had always associated the marriage act with something nasty. "I had forgotten that, and despite all the things I heard and read to the contrary, my emotional reaction was not what my brain told me it should be. To have that thing up and out where I could look at it, see it for what it was, was like getting a big lump out of my throat."

To a large extent we know ourselves through our relationships with others. If no one has ever loved me, how do I know I am lovable? If no one has ever trusted me, how do I know I am trustworthy? If I have never been loved or trusted, how can I love myself, how can I trust myself? The self-doubts, the inadequacies which we see in ourselves, as man or woman, are part of the human condition. But love, the deep love-commitment of marriage "for better or for worse," can drive out such fears.

Much of the confusion and suffering that mars man-woman relationships, whether in marriage or not, is rooted in fundamental misconceptions regarding what manhood or womanhood is. Despite all the frankness regarding sex in our movies, books and conversations—and in part because of some of it—many people remain confused and troubled regarding their own sexuality. Their relationships with others are clouded by their personal confusion.

One major misconception that proves most troublesome is that which thinks of our sexuality solely in terms of our genitals. In this case, sex education becomes a course in basic anatomy, a description of the generative organs and menstruation process and a diagramming of how babies are conceived and born. Marriage manuals are, often enough, only guides to the physiology of the body and the mechanics of sexual intercourse. Sexual relations—in this context—means only genital relations. All too many such guides approach the whole mystery of the man-woman encounter in marriage not as a matter of the adjustment of two unique persons to one another's style-of-being but to a matter of positions taken during sexual intercourse. More than one marriage counselor had been confronted by a couple whose major difficulty stemmed from a book which had led them into the trap of looking at their marriage partner as a sexual object whom they self-consciously manipulate rather than as the person they love, to whom they bring the fullest expression of their love.

This mistake of equating sexuality with genitals only is rooted in another: that of thinking sexuality is something we *have* rather than the expression of who we *are*. And from this often flows another misconception, that sexuality is a matter of role. This attitude would have us believe that being a man or a woman is a matter of hair style, costuming, a set of clearly defined interests and, especially, a certain way of thinking and acting; all of which are imposed upon us from without rather than flowing from within.

Often enough this definition of our sexuality as a part we must play in a drama scripted by others begins in the crib—blue blankets for boys and pink ones for girls; it is carried on with remarks like "Nice girls don't do that," or "Big boys don't cry," "Dolls are for girls," "Baseball is for boys." Even within the childhood milieu itself there is peer group pressure on the child so that playing or working with members of the opposite sex is "sissy" or "tomboyish." In the past this was reinforced on the adult level by voting and job discrimination practiced against women, and was even incorporated into laws which did not allow women the same legal rights as men.

While much of this legalized depersonalization of women is past history, the residue of such attitudes persists. The divisions of play and work into categories suitable to men and women are not yet entirely behind us. A woman truck driver remains a fit subject for a news item, and women still suffer the liability of being excluded from certain vocations, such as the ministry. Some still define masculinity in terms of brute strength, of baseball talk and aggressiveness, and femininity in terms of docility, emotional weakness and fluttery indecision.

In recent years a feminist movement has arisen which is second only to that which, in an earlier part of this century, brought the vote to women. A spate of books has appeared in which women authors roundly condemn their imprisonment in a "role." Unfortunately, many of them in trying to put down one misconception foster another. The thesis of some of these books is that there simply are no differences at all between men and women; in striving to make a statement for equality as persons, some insist on the sameness of the sexes.

In order to make such a case, these authors usually use as their touchstone the masculine job, or work ethos, and talk in terms of wifely careers, economic independence from the husband. Often while commencing their argument by denouncing the role playing of the sexes, they end up themselves urging upon their readers merely a new role to play. Not only do they thus fall into the very snare they wish to warn against, but often enough endorse another misconception: that our identity as persons, man or woman, is discovered through our job.

The feminists of yesterday and today are quite correct in protesting the easy generalizations which put man down as "active, aggressive, intellectual" and woman as "passive, tenderly receptive, intuitional or emotional." In every man worthy of the name there are what have been called "feminine traits" and in every woman "masculine traits." The variations, the quality and degree of pronouncement of these traits due to genetic and environmental background, psychological and educational development, differ in each of us. It is wrong to imprison women in a cage which says they are not to use their brains, are being unfeminine if they head up corporations, just as wrong as it is to say that men are being unmanly if they weep when full of grief or if they choose to become ballet dancers.   •

This is not, however, to say the sexes are the same. The role playing, the easy generalizations, are the exaggerated outgrowth of real differences in styles-of-being between men and women. A concrete example from our experience might help clarify this.

A woman neighbor of ours had the shock of discovering her infant dead in his crib. She ran screaming into our home. After verifying the infant's death, Clayton called the coroner and took charge of the necessary details while Myra consoled the bereaved mother. At the woman's request, Clayton called her husband. This man, a veritable tiger of the aggressive masculinity portrayed in certain men's magazines, had deserted his wife shortly after she had become pregnant. Informed of the tragedy, he said no, he didn't want to talk to his wife because he could hear her crying in the background. Then he hung up. We called her minister, who came and stayed with her a while, praying with her and consoling her. Her husband came the next day, stayed a few hours and left before the funeral. "I told him to go," the woman said. "I couldn't carry him as well as myself through this."

Another neighbor inquired: "What sort of man is that?" He got the reply, "No sort of man at all."

Later, the woman spoke of the half hour with the minister and how he had helped her through the ordeal. "I don't know," she told Clayton, "what I would have done without you and him to lean upon. You men gave me strength."

Her husband would be enraged or dumfounded to think that the gentle, soft-spoken minister or the nonpugilistic author was more of a man than he was. His own wife, however, had said just that. For if there is one quality that a woman desires from her man, it is strength. Not the animal strength so much glorified in our men's magazines and John Wayne movies, but the moral strength that means a woman can repose her faith in this man and not have it betrayed.

The woman mentioned could manage alone. She continues to manage alone, but she doesn't like it and is crucified by it. Managing alone means that she lacks the freedom to be fully feminine, that she has no man upon whom she can depend in time of trial. For there is a dependency, it seems to us, in the psyche of woman, a dependency only hinted at and in a sense manifested by her very physical dependency during pregnancy and nursing that demands as its counterpart a dependable human being.

Another recent event illustrates something of the quality of this strength that we would call the masculine style-of-being. A husband suffered a long-drawn-out death agony from cancer. For the last months of his life his wife nursed him day and night with unflagging devotion and tenderness. After his death someone praised her heroic care for her husband during those excruciating months when he was much of the time unconscious or babbling and all of the time smelling of the disease. She replied with calm certitude: "I couldn't have done it alone. It was his courage and strength that carried me through."

Part of the neofeminist movement would seem rooted in the fact that all too many men have broken under the fears of the age, have proved themselves undependable, less than manly when it comes to the strength that counts. At the same time much of the male uncertainty of our day is based upon the female lack of surety about who she is, her lack of confidence in her man. For if the man is meant to be a rock of strength, dependable, a man of moral courage in confronting the world, the woman must help him to be that. Her strength is as necessary to their relationship as is his own. Hers is a different kind of strength, not inferior, just different. Her strength must be in a certain moral courage that leads her to have faith in her husband, to place her loyalty to him above all others, save God.

An example of what we mean by this occurred some years ago. An established corporation lawyer, with the commodious home and two cars that went with his position, reached the conclusion that he wanted to become a psychologist. This meant uprooting his wife and four children, going halfway across the country and undertaking a student's life once more. His wife was torn by the pull of friends and relatives and her love for her husband. "He can't do this to you," they counseled. "You've been through that struggle once. You must demand your rights." These promptings echoed some of her own feelings, but she was also aware that this was in a sense the deepest test of her wifely love for him. By refusing to go, by insisting on her rights, she could stop him from pursuing this new goal, but only at the cost of stunting his growth. Here, she saw, was a great opportunity to show her husband the faith she reposed in his good judgment and abilities.

Having made the decision, she made it a wholehearted one. She gave full support to his efforts, kept him from discouragement, in every way provided the rooting section the flagging spirits require. Today her husband is one of this nation's leading marriage counselors. By strengthening his confidence in his own good judgment, she helped him fulfill his hopes, grow in manliness. In that same action she also grew in womanly love. Her trust was not betrayed, she is ever stronger in that confidence. And not only their own marriage, but literally thousands of other marriages are the happier because of her wifely love.

We can't overestimate the importance of this need in a woman for a strong man upon whom she can depend, nor upon the need in a man for the dependency, the faith-act, of a strong woman. One of the sorry by-products of overemphasis upon the individual rights of marriage partners today is that it is directly at war with this mutual dependency. Marriage is based upon that mutual surrender of rights to one another, and the healthy marriage is one in which the matter of "rights" and "duties" never comes up because the commitment is lived out not as a contract, but as a love affair, a constant gift-giving to the other.

So dependent upon one another are man and woman that we cannot even think of masculinity and femininity separately. The being of man is toward woman, his very masculinity has meaning only in regard to her, even as the being of woman is toward man, her femininity needs a man. Each is but half of the equation that makes up humanity; each helps the other attain wholeness as a person.

Perhaps it is only in theology that we can get a clear vision of the reality, the mystery which we are discussing. For both men and women find their identity in the realization that they are children of God. From the first their relationship as man and woman was meant to be one of mutual completion. She was to help him, to make up for his lack, and to bring to fruition in him qualities of mind and heart that could never exist without her. Similarly, he was to help her, to enrich her with the fullness of womanhood, to remove from her the curse of the barren womb.

According to Jewish teaching, husbands are to honor their wives more than themselves and treat them with tender consideration. Judaism sees marriage as a sacred trust that affects the couple's thinking and whole way of life and as a result creates a spirit of holiness that transforms their home into a small sanctuary.

In the Christian dispensation the husband's headship is described as like to the Headship of Christ over his Church. This carries with it the meaning that he is to sacrifice himself on his wife's behalf, to aid her to develop all her talents, to encourage her in all her efforts at self-identity, to sustain her in times of trial, to make fruitful their relationship. Because he is willing to do this, she on her part is freed from the need to be masculine, she can rest upon him as the foundation stone of her life, not in passive resting, not as moss on a rock, but as the Church rests its faith in Christ, ever growing, ever developing, ever bringing forth new fruits of life.

For, if man and woman bring themselves to one another at the time of their exchange of vows, if they then begin to actualize a further dimension of their beings in becoming husband and wife to one another, they also bring to their wedding their potentialities for motherhood and fatherhood. Whether this is, in fact, in a particular marriage actualized, the fact is that every marriage of man and woman is open to this further ripening of their beings. For fatherhood is the crown of manhood and motherhood the mature fulfillment of womanhood. Openness to this potential fruitfulness is openness to the future of their love, to God's will in their lives. The commitment to the other includes: "I want you to be the father of my children," "I want you to be the mother of my children."

Even should a marriage be childless, the openness of that marriage in generosity to the will of God, to the needs of the community of God's children, shall be the secret of its happiness. For there are biologically childless couples who have been father and mother to thousands, even as those who have made themselves "eunuchs" for the sake of the Kingdom are called Father and Mother. The touchstone here is unselfish love, openness to God's gifts of life.

In the final analysis, the man-woman relationship, if it remains only that, is a sterile encounter. It is fraught with the fear of death, for if each has only the other, then all is lost when the other is gone. But the encounter of man and woman has an end beyond itself and that is their mutual encounter with God in each other. It is when the man and woman have discovered him as the source of their unity and joy—and also as the fullness of bliss toward which they strive—that we can say that these two become truly one in marriage.

2

Your Family Heritage

•

THERE IS MUCH TALK of a "generation gap" today. There is, no doubt, a generation gap, but it is far from new. Fathers and sons confronting one another from a different ground of values have featured widely in the world's literature as part of the human condition. And when Cro-Magnon young men were drawing their sketches of the bison hunt on the walls of the Altamira Caves, there was surely some elder about grumbling: "What on earth is this younger generation coming to . . . wasting time drawing squiggly lines when there are stones to sharpen for tomorrow's hunt?"

If the tension between generations is not new, it is today, without doubt, wider than ever in the past. Consider for a moment the experienced reality of life as it appears to the present parental generation and their newly adult offspring. For the sake of brevity let's merely look at Daddy and his son, Junior. With slight variations it applies to Mommy and Jane as well as the other children in the family.

Daddy was born just after World War I. His parents and teachers were people who were born in the nineteenth century. At an early age he, therefore, learned from people for most of whom religion was a matter of rigorous obedience to the letter of the law, sex was the work of the devil, nationalism was a virtue, pleasure was usually a sin, a successful man was a wealthy one, imperialism was the "white man's burden," a woman's place was in the home, a good father was the man who provided well for his family's material needs.

When he was in his teens, the depression hit Daddy's world. His father lost his job and sought work anywhere, finally on W.P.A. The family was thrown very much together. In the next few years Daddy helped his mother pull the wagon to the relief store for a sack of cornmeal and another of potatoes. He took a magazine route and the money he earned went into the family fund, while the "Brownie" and "Greenie" coupons were saved up for a bicycle which, when he got it, permitted him to carry a paper route. Men came to their back door asking for a sandwich in exchange for odd labor. When Daddy was seventeen, he was able to buy a broken-down Model A for twenty dollars and after months of work had a moving vehicle. He went into the Civilian Conservation Corps when he was eligible and a portion of his earnings went home to support the family.

Then on a clear Sunday morning the war came. He went. Few questioned the rightness of his going. Even those, like the movie actor Lew Ayres, who were "conscies," were so not because the war was unjust but because they personally would not kill. The moral question was not raised to Daddy's generation. The Japanese aggressor who had ruthlessly bombed the American fleet, the German aggressor who was ravaging Europe and killing millions of defenseless men, women and children, had to be stopped. He went to war and was a good soldier. When the atomic bombs raised their mushroom clouds over Japan, he sighed with relief. A long and bloody conflict was at last over.

Daddy came home, took up life with the girl he had married on leave. A grateful country—also concerned about what dumping over ten million men on the labor market might do to the now booming economy—gave him the GI Bill. He knew the value of education; depression had taught him that. Why, one service station chain during the depression had hired only college graduates to pump gas! A good job was crucial, for it meant money. Without money you starved. So he went to school.

As he was a good soldier, so he was a good student. His wife worked to supplement the GI Bill and earned the PHT, "Putting Hubby Through," diploma. Their first child was born within a year of his homecoming. They desired to make up for lost time, to settle into normal life. Junior's major virtue was to be quiet while Daddy studied. Television helped with that. Daddy and Mommy, after the deprivation of the depression and the scarcity of the war years, were delighted with installment buying. Signs extolling the advantages of buying now and paying later had replaced the older ones: "Do Not Ask for Credit." They bought. Not having much time for him, they bought especially for Junior. Money was valuable, and so gifts—such as they had not had at his age—showed their love for him.

After graduation the family moved to a new tract on the GI Bill and thought it just lovely as Daddy went off to his chosen profession. He worked hard there, too, making up for lost time in building up his career. He brought work home, spent Saturdays on the golf course with helpful business associates and prospective clients. They moved twice more and today reside in a forty-thousand-dollar home and have two cars . . . and worry about Junior. "I can't get through to him," Daddy complains. "He doesn't appreciate what we've done for him."

Junior's history tells the story. Born in 1946, he was raised according to Dr. Spock. His parents were health-conscious and he's never wanted for the best medical care from the time of birth. They gave him material gifts they had not had and his money came from an allowance. He never *had* to work at all and, indeed, jobs were hard to get on a part-time or summer basis. Even if there was no cash, there was always the credit card in the glove compartment of the car which he got to use.

On a deeper level, Junior has lived with the specter of the draft confronting him since he was old enough to remember. There will be a weeding-out process at eighteen. How many decisions can one make about the future when that imponderable is present? So the now is very important. Daddy's emphasis on education for a job misses the point. Jobs don't count anymore. It's what I want to do with my life that counts. Daddy's emphasis on money doesn't count because Daddy and Mommy have money and they aren't that happy. Besides Junior has never seen anyone starving to death in our welfare state. So he tries to talk about possibly not going to war, or about not thinking about what he's going to *do* with his education, or about any number of things and finally says of Daddy, "I just can't get through to him."

Succinctness has ruled out giving all the subtle nuances of the situation, but this brief description helps demonstrate how our separate histories influence our approach to life. It serves to clarify some of the situations that develop not alone between the parental generation and their newly mature children, but also between husband and wife. For just as wide as the gap between Junior and Daddy can be the gap between a young man and woman raised in the same society, but in different families.

As human beings, we are rooted in time, have been born to certain parents at a certain time and place. The family life we grew up with, whatever characteristics it might share with other families, was unique in its interplay of emotions, attitudes, relationships. Likewise, as part of that family, we came into contact with the larger world through it, met certain other families, had certain playmates, went to a certain school. A man and a woman approaching the altar of marriage wish to donate their total selves to one another. The selves they offer is the sum total of their lives so far, the offering they make is of persons greatly influenced for better or worse by their personal histories.

Even their choice of each other is rooted in that heritage of the past. Consider the young woman whose father died when she was eleven. The girl was at that stage of development when her father was the "ideal man." Had he not died, her relationship with him would have undergone many changes which would have brought her to a more realistic understanding of him; but he did die. At thirty she was still waiting for the "right man" to come along, i.e., the man who could match her memory of her father in goodness, kindness, manly strength. Only when she was helped to realize that her ideal, patterned on her child's image, was unrealistic—that even her own father could not have matched her empedestaled idol—was she able to see her suitors as they were in themselves and, eventually, to marry one of them.

Or consider the situation of the young man who went through a period of adolescence and young manhood in which he chose to date only girls who were bland, indecisive, totally dependent and almost pitifully lifeless. However, he fell in love with a woman of lively personality and intelligence, a strongly individual woman. He found himself torn between what he had convinced himself was his type of girl and the reality of the woman with whom he had fallen in love. Although she was in love with him, too, he was torn by fear. His reason told him that they would be happy together, that she was more of a companion to him than any of the girls he had ever dated, but his instincts rebelled.

Honest questioning of himself confronted him with the reason: his mother was a strong woman with a massive thumb under which she had kept her husband and himself. He had for years looked down (not without guilty feelings) on his father as a weak man for permitting her to rule them both so dictatorially and had determined never to make that same mistake himself.

It was this determination which had caused him to avoid women he could not dominate. Now he saw that to marry one of his previous neurotically weak choices would have reversed the roles, but perpetuated the unhappy marriage of his parents. He saw, too, that his father was not without blame in the situation; that his weakness contributed to—perhaps provoked—his mother's tyranny. When he came to the conclusion that he was not his father and would not behave as his father, that the woman he loved was not his mother, that far from tearing down his manhood she was affirming it, that their marriage would be one of two unique persons determined to live their own lives, he was freed from the bondage of his fear and able to marry her. They are happily married today and proud parents because he learned from his personal heritage.

The couple exchanging rings often enough can only see one another. Everyone and everything else seems excluded from their view. Yet the presence of the two families at a marriage is testimony to the fact that in these two persons, two family histories have been joined. Even when the families cannot be physically present at the ceremony, the reality remains. None can deny the genetic facts testifying to this. In the couple will be found traces of the physical heritage of the past generations of the two families and we do well not to ignore the implications of that heritage on the spiritual, emotional, psychological, attitudinal formation of these two.

There is a significant difference, however, between the physical heritage and the heritage of environment and social conditioning which we bring to our marriage. Over the former, human beings have as yet no control. That one of us has blue eyes, the other green, that some of our children have blond hair, some black, some red, bespeaks a genetic heritage we accept as given. Over the heritage of our life experience, however, we can exert the control of our intelligence and our will. As human beings, we can look at our past history and seek to understand it; we can learn from it; we can weed out the destructive influences we discern there and affirm the creative elements.

If we have not reflected upon our personal history, consciously sorted out the influences of our heritage, then we are prisoners of that history. Each of us has a notion of the husband-wife relationship intimately linked with the reality of the marriage we were born into. Each received strongly rooted attitudes toward our own sexuality, toward family life in general, childbirth, breast feeding, discipline, from the family of which we were members. The marriage we lived with from the moment of birth, the family of which we were a member, provides us with the fundamental and, for many, the only marriage and family life "course" we've received.

As man, as woman, we are not perfect creatures. Whatever the vision of the beloved tells us, none of us marries the perfect mate. A realistic self-evaluation, a coming to grips with the realities of the past which have in one degree or another been the basis of our present attitudes, a mutual understanding of the conditioning of one another, are important if we are to make the adjustments that must be made to ensure a solid foundation for our marriage.

Unless this attempt is made, there is no foundation for communication. The most basic concepts of marriage may be at issue, husband and wife using the same words, each meaning something different. For example, he may mean by husband that —like his father—he's going to be settling into a routine of job, Wednesday bowling team, Saturday baseball game, evening beer and television, leaving his wife to manage the family budget, the shopping and all the housework. She may mean by husband that—like her father—he's going to take care of the monthly bills, spend Wednesday with the married couple's organization, take her dining and dancing more or less regularly, help with the dishes and chauffeur her to the supermarket. Because his father and mother never embraced or touched one another affectionately in front of him, and her father and mother displayed their emotional attachment often and freely, he may have the attitude that being married means an end to the effort of wooing her, while to her it means a constant nurturing of their love affair.

Even as it is crucial for father and son to understand one another's history as unique persons, so it is crucial to the husband and wife to do the same. Open discussion of their personal understanding of marriage and family life, the exchange of insights and attitudes, can help them to establish a common understanding of what they wish to build together. Without such mutual understanding, without shared ideals and shared insights into one another's past, we have the spectacle of two people trying to build a marriage from separate blueprints, separate concepts of what they are about, and constantly frustrating one another in the work.

Often the family heritage presses itself upon the bride and groom in the wedding itself. In recent weeks we attended three weddings, all of which were subject to the pressures of the family in a powerful way. In one, the young couple personally desired a simple ceremony, but the mother of the bride insisted on a full-scale formal ceremony. The couple decided to let her have her way and resigned themselves to unenthusiastically going through the formal paces for the benefit of a gathering largely composed of their elders.

Another couple, of which the groom was an artist, had designed their own wedding announcement, a tasteful but distinctly original invitation. The bride's mother insisted on the traditional, formal announcement. In the end the couple sent their card to their friends and she sent the traditional card to the relatives and her friends.

A third couple themselves assumed full responsibility for all arrangements; the parents were invited guests. The ceremony was attended by hundreds of their young friends as well as relatives and older friends. A nuptial mass, the music was furnished by a bearded bongo drummer and a sandaled and beaded bass player. The costuming was a brilliantly colored assortment, ranging from a Roman toga to the bride's Russian peasant dress. Instead of a wedding march, the congregation began to clap in rhythmic beat, ever more insistently, until the bride and groom reached the altar. With dignity, joy and beauty the wedding was truly celebrated. In every detail—such as the bride and groom embracing each communicant—the celebration was truly expressive of their style-of-being.

The impact of the family pressures brought varied responses to the wedding situation: one couple capitulated, one compromised, one went their own way. A case can be made for the couple who capitulated and the one who compromised with parental desires regarding the wedding ceremony as well as for the couple who went their own way. The apparent and obvious attempts to influence a couple must be met by the prudential choices of the couple involved. This happened in the case of the young couple who withstood the hysterics of a mother who thought her daughter was marrying a man with too little money and went ahead with their plans. The mother got off her "deathbed" to appear smiling and happy as the bride's mother at the wedding, but the father then tried to buy them a home, a car, and give the groom a job in his firm. The couple fled to Mexico for a year "until they understand we are an independent family and intend to live our own lives."

The open challenge presented by our families can be met openly, even by that leave-taking referred to in Genesis: "Therefore shall a man leave his father and mother and cleave unto his spouse." That leaving of father and mother can be taken in the most severe sense if it means preserving the marriage.

It is the other aspect of our family heritage, the pull of our background, that is less susceptible of easy answers. In fact, in many situations the attitudinal heritage, the psychological and emotional orientation, is only to be discovered as the marriage moves through history. As the children begin to grow, as matters of discipline, of education, of "cutting umbilical cords," require response, we begin to become aware of how deeply fixed that heritage may be.

But if we are open to the Spirit of God in our marriage, truly seeing the events and persons in our lives as challenges to growth, if we are aware that it is through our response to these new revelations of ourselves that we are meant to live more abundantly, then we will not be mastered by our heritage.

Far from being mere creatures of the past, we are, under God, the creators of our present. We are not mere slaves of our personal histories, we are involved in the making of history. And with all that has been said, if any of it be true, then we are also the ones who are in our marriage creating what our own children will in the future call their family heritage.

3

You

•

WE HAVE SOUGHT TO HIGHLIGHT some of the family influences, some of the understanding of our own manliness or womanliness which we bring to the wedding ceremony. But in both of these areas we hope we have made the point that there is nothing deterministic about our past experiences. Over them we have the task of judging, sorting, of integrating them into our personal lives in one way or another.

There are a number of people who function in our society on a day-to-day basis whose whole lives have been a surrender to some past experience: the alcoholic who blames his present state on the loss of his "dream girl"; the frigid woman who is still punishing herself and her husband for the brutality of her father; the man whose inability to communicate with his son is a repetition of his own experience with his father. There are some who have ceased to function entirely because of traumas of the past, and there are those whose traumas may have been as severe as any of the rest, but whose life-style seems the richer rather than the poorer for it. What really makes the difference in our lives is not so much the sort of experience one has, but the way in which we respond to that experience.

Two men can look at a daffodil and one sees only a yellow flower, while the other can write a poem revelatory of God's own beauty. Two queens heard the cries of the hungry; one went to them with armloads of bread, the other said, "Let them eat cake." The former was canonized, the latter had her head chopped off.

We've all heard the story of the two workers on the cathedral, both hauling heavy stones. Asked what they were doing, one responded, "I'm hauling this heavy stone over there." The other said, "I'm building a cathedral." Whether one is the pessimist who says, "The bottle's half empty," or the optimist who says, "The bottle's half full," it is not the bottle which has made us pessimistic or optimistic. Our response shows us to *be* the one or the other.

By working on our response, especially when it is a response we don't like, which makes us unhappy, we can change the beings we are. The man who looked on the daffodil and saw only the flower could, if he wished, apply himself to the poem written by his friend and the next time he saw the daffodil he might see something more in it. Had Marie Antoinette decided to emulate Queen Elizabeth of Hungary and carried a few armloads of cake out to the rabble, she would not only have gotten some good exercise, but may have discovered that they were sharers in her own humanity. Instead of being lifted to the guillotine, she, too, might have been raised to the altar.

Who is this you whose response is so important? When asked, how do you define yourself? Do you give your name? Do you say, "I'm a student," or "I'm a minister." "I'm ———'s son." Just for a few moments pause here and consider what, indeed, is your answer to the question: "Who am I?"

If your response has been in terms of your name, your sex, your job, your relationship with others, your race, your age, you've not quite told who you really are. Half of humanity is of your sex, surely the phone listings around the country have others with your name, and you really do exist when you are not studying or carrying on your job, don't you? After all, aren't you much more than your relationships with others? Aren't you more than a son to your parents, a boyfriend to your girlfriend, an employee to your employer, a student to your teacher? Don't you have a person-hood beyond these accidentals? In the final analysis must the response to the question not come down to "I'm me," which loads that "me" with all the meaningfulness which philosophy and theology can explore?

Not long ago, after a campus lecture, a young lady approached Clayton; he greeted her as one he had met the year before on a trip to the same campus. "I didn't expect you to remember me," she said. When asked why not, she went on: "Well, I'm plain and not very forward and I didn't say much that first time." Her words were faltering as she spoke, but finally she blurted out, "I just didn't think I was important enough to be remembered by anybody."

"But you're the only you in the world," Clayton responded. "There's nobody like you on the face of the earth, never has been and never will be again." Here was a young woman suffering from the sort of limitations of understanding that prompted another youth once to respond to the question "And who are you?" with "I'm nobody."

What you fundamentally bring to your marriage is nothing other than yourself: the who you are, the who you think you are. All of your attitudes toward your marriage partner, your children, your life circumstances, successes, reverses of fortune, the problems of your neighborhood and your world will flow from that understanding you have of yourself. It should be apparent that the person who has the ability to cope with new situations, work crises, new ideas and new people is the one who has confronted himself and accepted himself as worthwhile not for what he does, for how well he performs by the standards of others, for how much money he makes, but as worthwhile simply as the person he is.

There are many who, alone, find this task of self-confrontation difficult. Childhood traumas are buried deep, felt inadequacies are cloaked over with postures of superiority, fears of various kinds prevent self-discovery. A clinical psychologist who works mainly with young adults said of such people: "There comes the time when you've heard the story to the end. The young man has homosexual tendencies going back to parental attitudes from the time he was born, the young girl is miserable in her promiscuity which is a search for her father's love, or mommy was a drunk and the young woman is afraid of having a good time, or the home was a battleground and its main victim is now terrified of marriage. No matter what the situation, what brought them to me in their suffering, the point comes when you've got to put it to them: 'All right, that's how you got where you're at. That's why you're doing poorly in college, that's why you're afraid to marry. Do you like being this way? If so, what are you doing coming to me? If not, what do you intend to do about it?' "

This psychologist's approach is simply to point up our personal responsibility for the creation of the beings we are. We cannot pin the rap on someone else forever; we do have much to do with the direction of our personal lives. In all of our experiences, in our encounters with other people, in our looking at our own heritage, we have a multitude of choices to make which are a part of that ongoing process which we call life. None of us ever reaches the point where he can say, "I have finished growing. I am now mature." Life is meant to be a constant process of maturing and growth. Those who think and act otherwise are in need of therapy or burial.

The fundamental ground of our ability to love others is our ability to love ourselves. The Scriptures, in both Testaments, teach us in the "great commandment": "Love your neighbor as yourself." Only if I do love myself will I be able to understand the quality of the love for others which is commanded here. How does the normally healthy person love himself? Most important, he sees himself as irreplaceable. This vision of himself comes more readily, of course, if he is looking with the eyes of the man of faith. For then he knows that God called him into being as a unique, never to be duplicated person who has a place in the entire ongoing work of salvation history.

Aware then of his own dignity as a child of God, he respects himself. Aware of his calling to eternal beatitude, he is thankful for the gift of life, both now and forever. He senses a personal responsibility, too, flowing out of that relationship, a responsibility to shepherd creation, to build up the new earth in love and joy.

Of course, many who do not share this vision have a sense of their own worth. Most of us are quick to take care of ourselves, are care-full about ourselves, ready to say, "If you'd only see it from my point of view," or otherwise to rise to the defense of our egos, our rights, our property, when we think they are endangered.

Yet, when we look to the saints, to holy men like Rabbi Akiba, Francis of Assisi, or Gandhi, we find that their confidence of security in the hand of God freed them from such defensive attitudes. They were so busy about the task of loving others—they were always so aware of the dignity of others as unique sons of God that they showed respect to all they met and were more care-full about the people around them than about themselves. They were always ready to set aside their own egos when it was necessary to look at the situation from the other's point of view, to lay down their own lives in sacrificial love so that another might live more abundantly in their presence.

In doing so, of course, they were helping to create the people about them. They were saying to them, "You're worth it. I respect you. I love you. You are the center of my attention and not myself as I listen to you with my whole being." Such an attitude toward others is a literal living out of the command to "love your neighbor as yourself." And who is one's spouse, but the closest neighbor one is going to have? If a person does not have a proper love of self, how can he have the inner security necessary to show true love for the other?

The person who does possess this self-knowledge and self-love, which usually includes an ability to laugh at one's self (for a sense of humor is nothing more than a sense of perspective on events), is prepared for entering marriage. Such an integrated person, having accepted himself or herself, is first of all a free being: free to express himself, free from the fears of inadequacy, immaturity, the self-doubts which so many around him try to hide behind their armor of pride, arrogance or overbearing egoism.

Such a person uses his freedom responsibly: feeling responsible for himself and his actions, but also feeling responsible for the welfare of others whom he sees as another self, a person having as much subjectivity, as much feeling, as great a capacity for joy or sorrow as himself. When he says, "I love you," he is not saying, "I'm sexually hungry," or "You're good for me," or "Your strength (or weakness) feeds my neurosis," but rather he is saying: "I will your good."

Such a person is stable, not easily pulled off balance by the changing winds of circumstance, knowing that he is not what he owns, he is not what he does, he is not what others' opinions might make of him, but rather he is his own person. During the crash of '29 there were men who looked at the ticker tape as it told of their fortune's disappearance and cried, "I'm wiped out," then jumped out of a window onto the pavement of Wall Street. Such men identified with their money to the extent that when their money was wiped out, they thought they were finished. There are men in our society today who are undergoing immense inner stress because their jobs are being automated out of existence. There are women in our society who identified only with their role of mother and who, with the children raised, are bereft of a sense of purpose in life. The person who senses his own worth, founded on his appreciation of who he is, faces changing events, setbacks, and crises as challenges to be overcome and is not prone to see every wind of change or every new event as a threat to his existence.

Such a person is realistically open to the good and the bad in human life. His appreciation of the successes of others is untinged with envy or resentment because their success is no threat to his own self-esteem which is not grounded in these outside accomplishments. His denial of the bad, his working for the common good in his society, is rooted in his desire to see others have the same opportunities and advantages he has. Unlike some, he does not need anyone to look down upon in order to feel important.

Such a person keeps his word. We said such a person was "integrated," and integrity is rooted in that wholeness of the person. There is no need for him to play games; he has nothing to hide. Having accepted himself, he does not use masks. He is always at work trying to narrow the gap between his professed ideals and his practice of them, a continual task because, being human, he regularly fails. However, his honesty with himself permits him the freedom to be honest with others. He knows himself as human and to admit failure poses no threat to his being himself, since being human means failing from time to time.

Such a person is forgiving, aware of how patient God is with him, of how much in need of forgiveness he himself stands. He is well aware that his own forgiveness for his failings and trespasses will be in direct proportion to his willingness to forgive others their trespasses against him.

Such a person is not afraid of death or of life. His awareness of his humanity, his knowledge of who he is, is tied to the knowledge that he must one day die. He neither becomes morbid over this, nor does he flee from the thought. Indeed, this awareness makes him aware of the fragility of human existence. It casts into perspective the important and the nonimportant aspects of human endeavor. He enjoys life as the gift that it is, desires to share that gift, to help others to enjoy life. He is touched by the beauty of the world, especially by the beauty of men, women and children. On the other hand, he is well aware that here is no lasting city, that he is on pilgrimage to another city, one where the experience of life and love will be unimaginably more ecstatic in its piercing beauty.

When such a person comes to the altar, it is not with neurotic cravings about what he will get from this other, but in the fullness of desire to give himself away to the other. He is saying: "I will your good so strongly that I want to lay down the rest of my life for your sake." Greater love than this hath no man. When both partners to a marriage come to that moment of commitment in the same spirit, neither thinking in terms of rights or duties, in terms of what benefits will accrue from this, but only in terms of giving themselves away totally to the other, we are witnessing the start of one of those great marriages that shine forth as beacons to the world, upholding the message of life.

How much anguish would be saved how many people if, before marriage, they had come to grips with the problem of their identity, even more if they had the courage to ask themselves, "Why do I wish to marry? Why this person and not some other? What does he expect of me and what do I expect of him through marriage? Do we share the same ideals in regard to life, death, marriage, the world?"

Here are some reasons we've been given for getting married: "Because I wanted children." "Because I wanted to get away from my parents, and he was so sophisticated and witty in his remarks about them." "I was terrified of being an old maid and my mother liked him." "I was tired of the dating game and decided to settle down." "I wanted to quit work and have a home of my own and, well, he asked." "We kind of drifted into it, we had been going together for so long and it seemed expected." "I was pregnant by him."

In each case these reasons came from one party to a marriage that was on the rocks of divorce, separation or marital discord. In most cases the eventual difficulty was already visible before the marriage. The girl who had succumbed to the "If you loved me, you would" line had compounded the problem of being unwed and pregnant by marrying a person for whom love was a one-way street running only in his direction. She had gotten a husband who resented both her and their child for "trapping him" and "lousing up his life."

The girl who had married the older, more "sophisticated" man who had displayed such wit in ridiculing her parents and whose major offering was a passport away from home, found herself with a husband whose sophistication included the double standard and whose witty ridicule, now directed against her, was savagely sadistic.

The basic flaw in all the motives stated is the same. Each looked upon marriage as the solution to a problem they had rather than as the response to a person they knew. Each of the above reasons for getting married left out the only reason anyone should marry: the other person.

The response to the question "Why marry?" that does not come forth in the form of the name of the other person is a response one ought to question most carefully. The response which implies that marriage is the solution to some problem, the refuge after the storm, rather than the beginning of an entirely new adventure across uncharted seas which will have their share of storms demanding heroic self-sacrifice, ought to likewise be probed.

"Neurotics marry the neurotics they need" is an axiom of marriage counselors. One woman was for years the suffering and much-pitied wife of an alcoholic. This man finally decided to straighten out his life, went into therapy and, having discovered there the motivation for his drinking and seeing the unhappiness it caused himself and his wife, determined to quit. Six months of nondrinking on his part brought his wife into the therapist's office in a rage. "You've changed my husband!" she screamed. "You've ruined my marriage!" She had found personal satisfaction for years in the feeling of being morally superior to her husband, playing the role of the long-suffering wife among relatives and friends.

There are many who marry for the wrong reasons, whether neurotic or merely immature and unthinking. Persons yet unsure of their own identity marry one another in the hope of finding it through the other. This is possible, but more often than not it becomes a marriage of persons who, because they are strangers to themselves, are estranged from one another. Those who do marry for the wrong reasons, or in the hope that this will solve the problem of the alienation they experience in themselves, very often experience the first symptoms of their estrangement in their sexual lovemaking. How can the marriage act be an act of love if there is no authentic love present? Often enough these have the mistaken notion that their trouble lies in "how" they perform the marital act rather than in the "who" they married, and the "why" and "what" of marriage itself.

No amount of technical knowledge will make an act of love out of the sexual act that is not first of all the surrender of two whole persons, body-mind-spirit, to one another. Far more important than anything either is "doing" is the gift of the person that is being expressed. Each is enriching the other with the gift of his person. But the gift each receives is not only the other person, but the other person enriched and made more radiant with the love already given. Like the Gospel paradox that he who lays down his life shall save it, so in marriage, he who gives himself away is given back not only himself but himself enriched by the other.

One of the reasons there are so many marriage failures in our society is the ease with which marriage can be contracted. The civil requirements for contracting a marriage vary from state to state, but they are usually elemental. Each person must be of the age specified in that state as the age of consent; usually a slightly younger age is set for women than for men. A health certificate stating both are free of certain venereal diseases is usually required and a small license fee. A couple can then round up two witnesses (in some places the court or the Justice of the Peace will supply them) and the vows are exchanged. Obviously, it is not difficult to fulfill the legal conditions for marriage; the requirements for building a successful marriage are much more demanding. It should be apparent these requirements have little to do with the age of consent and a lot to do with understanding what one is consenting to. They have less to do with physical health than they do with psychological and emotional maturity. Much more important than the witnesses to the ceremony is the identity of the two persons who have brought themselves there.

We have all known people who, in making their marriage plans, select a church or synagogue wedding over a civil service—or vice versa—as if they were choosing whether they want ice cream on their apple pie. They seem to think of the religious or civil services as a matter of taste: "frills" or "plain."

The religious person is not one who sees religion as one slice of his life. If he is the integrated person we have been describing, his whole style-of-being is religious. There is little that he does, little that his life shows, that is not rooted in his awareness of his being the particular child of God he is, of his dependency upon God and his thankfulness which expresses itself in his responsiveness to the other members of God's family. Because he knows he does not depend upon himself, but upon God, he is stronger than most; because he knows he has more lives than only this one, he lives this one as if he has another.

For such a person a decision as serious as marriage is made prayerfully, conscientiously. He seeks God's will, knowing that God instituted the covenant of marriage, that unlike the other contracts which men can make or unmake as they choose, this covenant is unique and gains its strength from God and is meant to lead a man closer to the Father.

In the Old Testament matrimony was considered so holy that it was used as a metaphor for the relationship between God and Israel—God the bridegroom and Israel the bride.

In the New Testament the Christian understands the "two in one flesh" of man and wife as an imaging of the divinity and humanity of Christ brought together in one Person, and the dynamic living out of Christ's wedding with humanity in the Church.

If he considers marriage a sacrament, he understands it as a union which in a very special way is meant to bring God's love to the spouses through one another, each being bearers of God's own life to the other. He also sees that to be called to this state in life is to be called to lifelong witness to the most fundamental of Christian mysteries, Christ's wedding with humanity in his Church.

For the religious person, the wedding ceremony will be more than a spectacle, it will be a spectacular. It will be a moment when he and his bride say yes not alone to one another, but to God Himself. And when the yes said there is repeated in a thousand ways in the months to come, a million ways in the years to come, they will be conscious that the yes, uttered in exhaustion while answering the call of a sick child, murmured warmly into a pillowed ear, expressed in the grip of a hand at a time of crisis, is not only a yes said to the other but an affirmation to the call of God.

There are times, in the best of marriages, when the desire is present to withdraw the gift of self you've given. There are times of tears and hard words, times of loneliness and boredom, but even these, properly responded to, become times of growth for each, when they are seen as challenges to a more mature loving. For we are in the constant process of creating ourselves and, in marriage, we are always at work making or unmaking our marriage partner. If even our most casual encounter with another person is fraught with possible eternal consequences, what prodigious influences are we to effect on one another in the covenant of intimacy which is marriage?

In that creative work that we are carrying on with one another, which is an imaging out of the creative love of the Father for us all, there will be demanded of us a willingness to lay down our lives for the sake of the beloved in sacrificial love. But the creative and sacrificial love which we bring to bear will work not only to the sanctification of ourselves, our spouses and our families, but will radiate outward to all around us.

There is a print in our front room which was sent to us as a Christmas gift and which expresses much of this in a slightly different fashion. The picture is an abstract of red, orange, and yellow puffs like sunbursts above dry chaff, and written across the bottom are the words: "There are three things that keep life from being so daily—to make love, to make believe, to make hope, with the ordinary everyday people and stuff around us."

PART II

•

WHAT YOU BUILD
INTO YOUR MARRIAGE

4

The Shared Life

•

DAVID AND VERA MACE

David and Vera Mace are members of the Society of Friends. Over many years they have traveled to more than seventy-two nations, often in the capacity of consultants on family life to the World Council of Churches. They have conducted Family Life Institutes in Southeast Asia, Africa, the Caribbean, and most recently in Fiji for the Pacific Council of Churches. David wrote his doctoral dissertation on "Hebrew Marriage." He is one of the founders and the first Executive Director of the Marriage Guidance Council of Great Britain. Later he and Vera served as co-executives of the American Association of Marriage Counselors for seven years. At the present time David is Professor of Family Sociology at the Bowman-Gray School of Medicine, Winston-Salem, N.C.

•

"AND THE LORD GOD SAID, it is not good that man should be alone; I will make an helpmeet for him." So, in the Creation story, Eve was brought to Adam, and became his wife. His isolation was ended, and another had joined him to share his destiny.

Among other things, marriage is God's answer to man's dread of loneliness. The Church of England marriage service, listing the purposes which marriage serves, says that it was ordained in order that the couple might enjoy "the mutual society, help and comfort the one ought to have of the other." This answers one of the deepest human longings. It has been well expressed by the English writer Edward Carpenter:

> That there should exist one other person in the world toward whom all openness of exchange should establish itself, from whom there should be no concealment; whose body should be as dear to one, in every part, as one's own; with whom there should be no sense of Mine or Thine, in property or possession; into whose mind one's thoughts should naturally flow, as it were to know themselves and receive a new illumination; and between whom and oneself there should be a spontaneous rebound of sympathy in all the joys and sorrows and experiences of life; such is perhaps one of the dearest wishes of the soul.

In a study we made of life in the Soviet Union under Stalin, we found that the inner life of marriage became the last refuge of people living in constant terror. "When Vasili was alone with Elena, he found that he was now talking more openly than he ever had with anyone in all his life. Because they agreed on so many things, he got the feeling that, no matter what happened, he could trust her completely. . . . There sometimes comes into the mind of any Soviet man, no matter how loyal to the Government, a few thoughts which the police should never hear. In Russia if a man and woman love each other, he will always tell her such things." So marriage provides us with a place where we can unload our hopes and our fears, where we can speak of our highest ambitions and our most shattering disappointments, where we can take off the mask we wear before the world, relax and be truly ourselves. The shared life of marriage likewise provides us with encouragement and hope; so that we see the religious couple climbing the ladder to Heaven together, constantly helping and sustaining one another.

When a man and a woman of religious faith come to the threshold of the great experience of marriage, they will bring to it two deep convictions.

First, they believe that marriage is a gift to them from God, a blessing he has ordained. This is not true only of one or of several religions. It is a part of the order of creation, and belongs to all mankind. In the story of Adam and Eve, they were the parents of the entire human race, and not any particular section of it. The archaeologists, though they approach man's beginnings in a very different way from the Bible story, nevertheless come to the same fundamental conclusion—that as long as there has been man, there has been marriage; and a million years of man means a million years of marriage. Westermarck, in his monumental study of human marriage, came to the conclusion that it was a universal institution, always found wherever human beings lived together in a settled state of society. Marriage has, of course, existed in many varieties and patterns, but it seems that it belongs to our human nature. So the great religions of the world have seen it as part of the divine purpose, and have exalted it accordingly.

Secondly, religious people have the conviction that their personal choice of each other as marriage partners is not accidental or haphazard. In the beginning God gave Eve to Adam, and every son of Adam since, who has earnestly tried to live within the divine purpose, has believed that his particular Eve was given him by God. In the Old Testament days, when parents chose partners for their sons and daughters, they believed this profoundly. Here, in condensed form, is the story of Isaac and Rebekah from the Book of Genesis:

And Abraham said unto his eldest servant of his house . . . thou shalt go unto my country, and to my kindred, and take a wife unto my son Isaac. And he arose, and went. . . . And it came to pass . . . that . . . Rebekah came out. . . . And the damsel was very fair to look upon. . . . And the man bowed down his head and said, Blessed be the Lord God . . . : I being in the right way. . . . And Bethuel [her father] said, The thing proceedeth from the Lord: . . . Behold, Rebekah is before thee, take her . . . and let her be thy master's son's wife, as the Lord hath spoken. . . . And Isaac went out to meditate in the field at the eventide; . . . And Rebekah lifted up her eyes, and when she saw Isaac, she lighted off the camel. . . . And Isaac . . . took Rebekah, and she became his wife; and he loved her.

Notice how all the actors in the drama move in perfect harmony toward the goal they all share—to bring together the young couple according to the will of God.

What does this choice really mean? Plato, the Greek philosopher, relates an ancient myth which tells that in the beginning men and women were joined together in pairs, but that the gods in a mischievous moment tore them apart and scattered them. Thus it became the destiny of every man and every woman to seek out in the world his or her lost other half. This would hardly be our view of the matter. It is surely possible to succeed in marriage with a variety of suitable partners, and we know that the choice is determined by the possibility that two particular people will meet and will be available to each other. Yet most religious people feel, with a deep sense of conviction, that there is something special about the one partner a man or woman finally chooses. Anyone who believes that the great events of his life are divinely guided must feel in a special way that he needs to be sure of the will of God in making the choice of a marriage partner. For what choice of his whole life will hold so much significance for him as this one?

These are the foundations of married life for all religious people. Their creed is: "I believe in marriage as God's gift to me; and I believe that my choice of my marriage partner has been made within the circle of God's will for me."

So the choice is made, and the task of marriage begins. This marks a change of direction in the lives of the young people concerned. They began in a state of dependence, in constant need of their parents' help and protection. From this state they moved to independence, when they were free of binding relationships and able to move about without close ties. And now they have chosen to move back into dependence, or more properly interdependence, and must learn to live the shared life at a greater depth than they have ever before experienced it. André Maurois, the French writer, puts this well when he calls it a "formidable decision"—to bind oneself for life to search, not for someone who may please him, but to please the one he has chosen. Maurois insists that this decision alone can make a marriage succeed, and if it is not sincere, the couple's chances are very slim.

What *is* the task of marriage? Jan Struther, the English poet, talks affectionately in one of her poems to two young people who with youthful enthusiasm claim to be in love. She chides them gently for their presumption and tells them that they do not yet know what love really means. But they have "the raw materials of love"; and out of these, with enlightenment and perseverance, they may one day achieve the finished product. When two people move into marriage, what we need to imagine is a building lot cleared for construction and a pile of materials scattered about— concrete blocks, beams and planks, rolls of insulation, roofing shingles. The design of the house is clear to the builder because he has studied the architect's blueprints. But there is a great deal of work to be done before the pieces are all put together, jointed and fixed into position, and the finished house becomes a home.

So it is with marriage. As children, we loved to hear the fairy tales in which the handsome prince and the beautiful princess rode away together into the sunset, and the story ended with the words: "and so they were married, and lived happily ever after." And our childhood imagination saw them pass from the struggles of life, like earthly pilgrims entering Heaven, into a paradise of unending bliss.

We are no longer children, and we know that in real life it is not like that. Marriage is simply a part of human living, and it is not free from the pain and sorrow to which our mortal life is heir. Robert Louis Stevenson, the Scottish writer, warned his young readers rather grimly that marriage is more a field of battle than a bed of roses. Perhaps he was overpessimistic. Yet no one who knows what marriage is really like will deny that both the battle and the roses feature in the experience of most married couples.

A successful marriage normally passes through three stages. The first is a period of *mutual enjoyment*. This corresponds with the honeymoon stage. The word simply means "a month of honey." The couple go away together for a time (seldom as long as a month!) in order to enjoy to the full the experience of belonging completely to one another, to taste the sweetness of love without distraction in a setting of carefree relaxation. Not all honeymoons, as marriage counselors are aware, turn out just like that. But many do. And it is good for a couple to be able to look back, in the later years, on the beginning of their married life as an experience of sheer delight.

The second stage of marriage follows sooner or later—and sometimes all too soon. This is the phase of *mutual adjustment*. Now the time of dreaming is over, and the marriage builders turn from the blueprint to the piles of materials waiting in the yard. The task of making a marriage can be a very pleasant one, because work that is congenial is as satisfying in its own way as play. But it *is* work—make no mistake about it. Two different people, who for perhaps one-third of a lifetime have lived separate lives, are now coming together into a relationship of total intimacy and total sharing. It is unreasonable to expect that this kind of integration of two lives can possibly be achieved without the need for a few difficult, and even painful, adjustments. How could we expect two people coming together in marriage, however much they think they have in common, to be prefabricated to fit exactly the contours of each other's personalities? There must always be some sawing and planing, some cutting and filing to be done before they can fit their lives harmoniously together. And the less they have in common at the start, the more adapting they will have to do.

It is even more true that the more they are expecting from marriage, the more adapting they will have to do. And here we must face the fact that marriage today is much more difficult than it has been in the past. In earlier times, husband and wife had clearly defined roles in marriage. And these were planned so that the roles seldom overlapped or competed. The husband's main task was to "bring in the bacon." His work lay mainly outside the home, and he was the provider and protector. All he did around the house was the heavy work, and the mechanical jobs considered to be the exclusive province of males. The wife's sphere was inside the house, and here she took complete responsibility for housecleaning and maintenance, for cooking food and taking care of the children. It was a partnership, but they didn't talk of equality. Today, however, the roles of husband and wife have become more and more shared between them as marriage has become more and more a partnership of equals. Now men's roles and women's roles overlap; wives go out to work to help bring in the bacon, while husbands cook and change the baby's diaper. This brings them closer together, no doubt—but unless the closeness is managed with very good teamwork, it can stir up all sorts of conflicts that just didn't arise in the old-fashioned marriage patterns. We shall come back to this in the next chapter.

This brings us to the question: "How much of a shared life *is* marriage?" Out of the Bible account of the institution of marriage has come the idea of the *union* of husband and wife. So we sometimes talk in a rather ecstatic way about the two becoming one. This idea has a place in our legal system too, in the principle that husband and wife couldn't at one time give evidence against each other, because they were legally considered one person.

Of course two persons never can in fact become one. To talk about union, or even "fusion," of husband and wife is quite misleading. What the Bible says is that they become "one flesh"; and there is indeed an experience of merging into one another in the climax of the sex relationship, which we shall discuss later. But after sexual intercourse, they draw apart again, and are not in fact one flesh. And similarly, as persons, they keep their individual identity. To do otherwise would be unthinkable, because to merge them into one would destroy the unique individuality of each. Love does not wish to go as far as this!

In fact, in marriage husband and wife will strongly defend their separateness if they feel that it is in danger. This is something every loving couple must clearly understand. Dr. Van de Velde, whose book *Ideal Marriage* is well-known, wrote another book which few people have read, called *Sex Hostility in Marriage*. In this he suggests that between men and women there is an age-old fundamental hostility—a theme many writers have discussed. There may be something in this. But in our opinion, much of the evidence quoted from marriage to illustrate this theory really arises from the natural defense of the individual ego against being too much confined and closed in by the demands of the marriage partner. In marriage you must respect your partner's right to a reasonable amount of separateness and even solitude. "Let there be spaces in your togetherness," says Khalil Gibran, the Lebanese poet.

What then should the young husband and wife expect of marriage as they start out on the task of building their relationship? This is an important question, because expectations may well decide whether or not the partners consider their marriage successful. In a study we made of marriage in the Orient, written up in our book *Marriage: East and West*, one of our major findings was that in Eastern lands people have tended traditionally to expect less of marriage than it can reasonably be expected to offer; whereas in the West, so influenced by rosy romantic concepts, expectations have been unreasonably optimistic. What this means is that most people were satisfied with what marriage brought them in the East because they didn't expect much; and therefore marriage tended to be very stable. But in our Western culture, the high level of expectation has risen so much above what is in fact attainable that large numbers of people soon become disillusioned and want to divorce their partners and try again, in the hope of doing better next time. It is thus true to say that an exaggerated idealism about marriage is one of the major causes of divorce.

Happiness or success in marriage is, therefore, very much a function of expectation. We could even imagine two married couples, living next door to each other in exactly identical conditions, and yet one couple could think themselves happy and the other consider themselves unhappy in their married life, simply because their expectations had been widely different. An attempt was in fact made in a research project to test this out and the evidence tended to confirm it.

It is important, therefore, that while married couples look to the stars, they should also keep their feet on the ground. Let's be realistic, and face the fact that probably only a small proportion of all men and women are highly endowed with the qualities we define as "marriageability." Moreover, these people won't necessarily get married to each other, so a lot of married people are going to bring to marriage only moderately good qualifications for the job, and to find similar limitations in their partners. If these people are expecting or demanding the highest levels of married happiness to come to them quickly and with little effort on their part, they are certainly doomed to disappointment. Marriage is a splendid institution, and has much to offer us; but it is not exempted from the universal fact of life that you seldom get something for nothing. We shall do far better, as married couples, if we accept this fact at the start, and recognize that marriage is indeed a deeply rewarding experience, but only for those who will accept it as a task and put in the necessary labor to reap the rewards in due season.

We would go further. It has been our impression, through long years of counseling with thousands of married people, that the best marriages of all are not necessarily those in which husband and wife began by being ideally suited to each other, and made all their adjustments quickly and with little effort. There are indeed such marriages. But we have been surprised when very happily married people have given us their confidence to discover how many of them had come at last to a rich and deeply satisfying relationship only after earlier years of struggle and conflict. And we find that people value a rewarding marriage all the more when they have achieved it only after much suffering and sacrifice. The struggle to make a marriage work has been for some people the most maturing experience in their entire lives. We feel that religious people, who regard highly the sanctity of married life, can sometimes bring such resources of faith and perseverance to bear in a difficult marriage that they can finally bring it to full fruition.

The shared life of husband and wife is complicated by the fact that in marriage we find not simply one relationship, but two relationships coexisting side by side. Failure to see this fact clearly has resulted in incalculable confusion and trouble throughout human history.

First, husband and wife interact with each other as two persons in a partnership. Marriage has not always been viewed as a partnership, but this concept is now very widely accepted in our modern world. As partners, husband and wife are considered equals; and we shall look at the implications of this in the next chapter. Their partnership compels them to face all the problems that arise whenever two human beings become involved in a shared enterprise. This may at times severely test their capacity to handle differences of opinion; and it is not to be expected that any two people, however well matched and however much in love, will always and inevitably want to do the same thing in the same way at the same time. Disagreements are therefore bound to come, and they put the partnership of the marriage to the test. Only by a process of gradual adaptation to each other can the partnership become smooth and effective. This process of adjustment should be, of course, already well started in the engagement period before marriage; but in the greater closeness and continuity of married life it is usually intensified, and young couples need to be ready for this.

While they are learning to be partners, these same two people will also be dealing with another and quite different relationship between them. This is their interaction as male and female, as masculine and feminine. This relationship has a completely different foundation from the other. As partners they are equals; and nowadays we hear much talk about the "fifty-fifty marriage." But equality simply has no meaning in their masculine-feminine relationship. Here, what is important is not their likeness to each other, but their difference from each other. We say they are *complementary*—each brings to the other something the other lacks, and something the other needs. Just as they "fit" each other physically, because their sex organs are different but complementary, so they "fit" each other emotionally as well. But achieving this emotional complementarity in marriage is not always an easy task. All kinds of complications can arise, as every marriage counselor knows. The couple have to come to terms with their sexual needs in the direct sense, and with all the more indirect features of their difference in gender, such as dependency needs, role differentiation, and reciprocal interaction. We shall be looking at some of the practical implications of this later.

How long does the adjustment period of marriage last? There can be no general answer to that question. Variations seem to be very great. There are couples who do a great deal of their adjusting before marriage, and come to married life so well prepared that the process of adaptation goes so smoothly that it is hardly noticed. On the other hand, there are couples who find the marriage-building task really rough, and have to struggle on with it for years, yet emerge in the end as very happily adjusted husbands and wives. Probably the first year of marriage is the critical year, because by that time couples have usually developed habit patterns of interaction that tend to be repeated over and over in the years that follow. If these are good patterns, the marriage progressively develops. If they are bad patterns, the marriage degenerates.

The real tragedy is that in so many marriages the task of adjustment is never realistically faced. We do in general such a poor job of marriage preparation that some couples don't even see marriage as calling for a process of adjustment at all. And of those who do, many are so poorly equipped for it that they soon get discouraged and give up. What then happens is that they simply seal up those areas of their relationship in which they are unable to achieve adjustment, and try to make the best of what remains. It is as if a bunch of ham-handed builders made such a botch of putting up a house that when the family moved in, there were only a couple of rooms that they could live in comfortably. It is these incomplete, weak, mediocre marriages that become readily susceptible to breakdown when they are subjected to periods of special tension. There are very many of them in our contemporary culture; and most are destined a few years later to contribute to the divorce statistics.

It would be our judgment that practically all marriages that fail do so because they are unable to cope with the tasks of the adjustment period in marriage. Many of these actually break up in the early years. But even when marriages fail later in life, there is almost invariably evidence that the inadequate adaptation of the earlier years has at last caught up with them. When the wind blows through the orchard it is the unhealthy apples, rotting from within, that fall. And it is likewise the marriages that have failed to achieve healthy patterns of managing the shared life that, sooner or later, collapse.

If the tasks of marital adjustment are successfully carried out, the couple move into the third stage of *mutual fulfillment*. This lacks the ecstatic quality of the honeymoon period, which can never be experienced again. But in a deep and less exciting way it is just as satisfying. And the satisfaction is enduring. For, once a marriage has reached this stage of mellow maturity, it is not likely to be threatened by failure. Now the couple have come to the point where they know each other completely and have accepted each other completely.

They know how far they may provoke each other; and how far they had better not provoke each other! Each knows how much the other can give, and what the other is unable to give. Probably all the dreams have not been fulfilled. But the couple have learned the art of living together in mutual cooperation and mutual support; and this is so much better than anything else life seems to offer that they are thankful for the blessings they share and want to go on sharing life as long as life continues.

5

Communication and Conflict

•

ONE HOT EVENING IN INDIA SOME YEARS AGO, we were talking to an invited group of young women about modern marriage. In spite of the heat and in spite of the complete novelty of the subject from their point of view, they were entirely relaxed, particularly when we reached the point of trying to describe to them what marriage counseling is and what it aims to do. In fact they were so relaxed that it was very clear we weren't communicating with them, although they were much too polite to say so.

We decided on a new line and asked, "Tell us, what happens in your country when husband and wife quarrel?" They smiled indulgently at our ignorance and replied, "Oh, that doesn't happen." Clearly, we were not getting our question home and must put it differently. "Well, what happens when the husband and wife do not agree about things concerning their marriage relationship, their life together, and their family?" The relaxed mood passed, and with one strong united voice they said all together, "Oh, *that* never happens."

With urgency, we demanded to know how and why. This is what we learned. From her earliest childhood the Indian girl is (or should we say "was"?) brought up knowing that one day her parents will arrange a marriage for her, and that the man she marries will be as a god to her. In other words, he can do no wrong, and she must worship, if not his actual person, at least his acknowledged superiority and infallibility. Hence, the Indian wife cannot quarrel with someone who is always right; she cannot disagree with an infallible husband. Because she has been brought up to accept this situation without question or challenge, conflict in her marriage is simply not a possibility for her. At best she conforms to the pattern throughout all her life. At worst, she endures to the end because, as our young friends explained to us, if she reaches a point where she can no longer bear it, she cannot end the marriage, therefore all that is left to her is to end her life.

In Westernized urban centers in India, as in other parts of the world where patriarchalism has been the pattern since time immemorial, situations are rapidly changing today. But nowhere do young people find themselves in such great dilemmas concerning communication and conflict in marriage as in our Western culture.

In the first place, whatever traditional marriage patterns there were in the past have largely been abandoned. Even many of our churches today have relaxed their teaching of the indissolubility of marriage, and no longer are wives and husbands virtually compelled to endure marital conflict whatever the cost. No longer do strife-ridden marriage partners have the stability of tradition and the consolation of custom to act as a kind of collective scaffolding around their individual marriages.

Secondly, young people today want it the way it is. We wrote in the last chapter about expectations in marriage. Young people today mostly enter marriage with high hopes and great expectations, and generally strong belief in their capacity to achieve these. This is fine. These are the materials out of which the sturdy and strong house of marriage may be built. And what Dr. Alfred Kinsey, the well-known American social scientist, called "the will to make it work" is the greatest single material, humanly speaking, of all. Dedicated to God, this can be lifted beyond our human limitations.

We would say, on the basis both of our personal experience and of observation, that the fundamental key to building a good marriage is to establish at the beginning and maintain at all costs completely open lines of communication between husband and wife. For religious men and women, this means being as open to one another as they are individually open to God. This is a concept of marriage that many people would reject outright. And many who would accept it as a good idea in theory would hesitate to put it into practice. In the eyes of some it appears as a policy full of dangers. We are aware of both the difficulties and the dangers. We are even prepared to admit some exceptions to the rule and will discuss them later. But, as a working principle, we are convinced that it is the foundation stone of the really successful marriage.

The fairy tales can mislead us about marriage, but nevertheless homespun truths are hidden here, and at least at one point they offer us some very sound advice. In some of the stories, after the prince has rescued the fair maiden from the jaws of the terrible monster and the crisis is over, the couple sit down pleasantly together and talk. And the story says of the prince: "And he told her all his heart."

Good marriage *depends*, above all else, on good communication. And it's an excellent plan to start as you mean to continue. We knew one engaged couple who did this very thoroughly. One evening each week, they drove out to a hillside parking place that commanded a sweeping view. There, in the parked car, for hour after hour, they took turns at telling each other their whole life stories. The rule was to begin with the things that were hardest to tell. By the time they were finished, they felt they knew everything that mattered about each other. They knew exactly whom they were marrying—no unpleasant surprises lay ahead.

This is harder for some people to do than for others. But all married people have to understand that the intimate life of marriage is something quite different from the wider social relationships we have with friends, neighbors, and business colleagues. In that wider life we don't reveal our inner selves. We try to project a good image, to keep up appearances. And we don't probe into the personal affairs of the other fellow. We are polite, but evasive. This is appropriate, because we don't plan to enter into relationships in depth with these people.

In other words, the pattern we adopt in these social relationships is not based on telling the truth, but on keeping appropriate distance. When an acquaintance asks, "How are you?" you automatically reply, "Fine." In fact you may have many aches and pains and afflictions. But that's no business of his, and you are not about to discuss your ailments with him. If you stop to think about it, you realize from your own experience that even the question is probably false, a mere convention, and so you give him an answer that is in fact a lie. Or if a tiresome business contact calls you to ask for an appointment, you reply in honeyed words that you'd be delighted to see him, but unfortunately your schedule is full right up for a week ahead. In fact this is not strictly so, because an hour later you "manage" to make an appointment with the vice-president of a firm with which you're doing important business.

There's nothing iniquitous about these devices. They are just patterns of communication designed to protect your privacy and to keep troublesome people away. But if you take these patterns of communication into marriage, you will soon be in trouble. You just can't run the shared life without open and honest communication. Yet many couples try to do so; and the tangles they end up in are almost unbelievable.

As we said earlier, there are exceptions to the rule of open communication in marriage. They are of two kinds. First, the confidences of a third party must be strictly kept. When we are involved in counseling, for example, it is understood between us that, unless the client has voluntarily given us permission to do so, we do not share with one another any confidences given to either of us. Similarly, married persons, as part of their duty to their relatives and friends, must continue, in their marriage, to exercise their obligation to receive and hold confidences in complete trust, with neither partner trying to force others' "secrets" out of his or her spouse.

The other exception concerns certain kinds of confessions. In general, the fact that a personal confession—perhaps of some sexual misdemeanor—is costly to make is a pretty good reason why it should be made. But this is not always so. A man who, for example, has been involved in a sexual affair with a friend of his wife might be eager to confess it, in order to get it off his mind and relieve his uneasy conscience. But in getting it off *his* mind, he may place a terrible burden on his wife's. When in doubt, we believe the right course is always to make the confession to a trusted third party—a priest or marriage counselor, for example; and then to arrive at a decision with the counselor as to whether the confession should be made to the wife. When the considered decision is that it would be unwise to tell the wife, the husband is safeguarded if later on the fact of the misdemeanor reaches her from another source, because the counselor can explain to her that the decision not to confess it was made with his knowledge and consent, and to spare the wife pain.

However, there are rare exceptions to the general rule. And the general rule is "Tell all." This takes time. Marriages may get into trouble, not because the couple are unwilling to open up to each other, but because weeks pass and there is no time to keep up to date. This is a serious matter, and should be treated as such. You can't keep a marriage in good repair without regular opportunities to report to each other. And "regular" should normally mean daily. If a time comes in a marriage when husband and wife feel no inclination to share their inner thoughts and significant experiences, that is as good an indication as any that they are drifting apart. If you can't naturally "let your hair down" with your marriage partner, it means your marriage isn't working to its full capacity.

The main purpose of communication in marriage is not to convey facts, but *feelings*. We all know that love expressed in words and actions is what keeps a marriage strong and healthy. But love is a positive feeling. What do we do with negative feelings when they arise, as they certainly do? In fact, problems nearly always focus on *negative* communication. When you feel angry or irritated with your wife, you bottle it up and say nothing. You may do this because the last time you spoke your mind you received a broadside of hostility in return, indicating probably that you went about it the wrong way. Hostile feelings against your partner should be communicated, but if possible not as hostility—rather as a concerned admission that there is a barrier between you at this point, and you want to talk it over in order to clear it up.

Or you may hold back your hostile feelings out of consideration for your wife because you don't want to upset her. It is highly probable that you will in fact upset her more by your strained silence and detachment than by unloading your hostility; because she will sense that you are upset, and she may very well jump to some imagined conclusion far different, and often more serious than the real cause.

You may even feel guilty because you *have* hostile feelings. This often happens to recently married couples. They have an ominous dread that if they allow anger to arise in their hearts, it will destroy their love. So they choke it back and try to pretend they don't feel it. All that happens is that they build up, deep down inside, a smoldering state of resentment that can be highly destructive to the partner in question and to the marriage.

We once counseled with a couple before marriage who fondly imagined that the mere fact of getting married would automatically deal with their conflicts. As the girl put it, "We fight like cat and dog now, but it will be different when we are married, won't it?" They were thinking in terms of the fairy-tale myth of living happily ever after, and how wrong they were!

At the root of all these difficulties lies conflict. Marital conflict is closely related to communication. Poor communication lies behind most serious conflict in marriage. And it is through improved communication that conflict is finally resolved. But it is very difficult for the couple to improve their communication by themselves while they are in a state of conflict. This is probably the main activity of marriage counselors—to help couples to break through communication deadlocks in order to resolve conflict.

Fortunately it is never too late to learn the skill of communication in marriage if both partners are willing. Many couples find their marriages springing into new life when a marriage counselor enables them to peel away the layers of evasion and deception in which they have almost stifled their relationship.

What *is* marital conflict? Young couples often view it with horror; as though it were an alien, menacing threat to their love, something from outside trying to break destructively into their relationship. This is a serious misconception, and it may have disastrous results. The couple may try to deal with conflict by shutting it out and running away from it. That is never successful —because the conflict is in fact not outside, but inside; and like pain in our physical body, it is a warning sign that health is threatened, that something needs to be attended to.

Let us look more closely at conflict in marriage, and see it for what it actually is. Its roots lie in the fact that people are different from one another. As we saw in the last chapter, husband and wife cannot expect to be alike in all respects; it would be a dull marriage indeed if they were. Difference in itself is not a problem in marriage. Sometimes it is the cause which makes people attractive to one another; as happens, for instance, when a girl falls in love with an exotic, mysterious foreigner.

But in the shared life of the marriage, difference comes out in disagreement. Disagreement is simply difference expressed in action, because each partner sees the situation in his or her own way, and consequently the policies they propose are in opposition to one another. When disagreements arise, and there is no apparent solution, angry, frustrated feelings are stirred up in each.

This is what we usually describe as conflict—a highly emotional state of mutual hostility.

What are you saying when you are in this state? In words, it would be something like this: "I am angry and frustrated because you are blocking my way to what I want to do. This is making me hate the person I ought to love. How can you treat me like this?"

Now, surely it is clear in the first place that this situation is bound to arise, over and over again, in *every* marriage. And it is also clear that this is not something to run away from—what good will that do? It is something to be honestly faced and resolved.

Social psychologists have taught us some helpful things about conflict. And one thing we know is that there are three ways of handling it—two of them unsatisfactory and the third satisfactory. The first way is for one of the marriage partners to insist on having his way by compelling the other to give in. Usually in a marriage one partner is more strong-willed and stubborn than the other. Traditionally the husband was the acknowledged boss, and the wife was expected to obey him in all matters. This was, in fact, a convenient way of avoiding conflict, by making marriage a one-vote system. Of course this was done at the expense of the wife's right to self-expression; but since women were expected to be subservient, they were used to giving in. Today, however, women are "emancipated," and many of them won't accept this obedient role. So it may happen that a strong-willed wife becomes in effect the boss, while her more easygoing husband habitually gives in. Either way, this is a poor way of dealing with marital conflict; because if this becomes a habitual pattern, it destroys the partnership and puts a kind of tyrant-slave relationship in its place.

The second way of handling conflict is for each to cling stubbornly to his or her position and refuse to budge. This means, of course, that the conflict is not resolved at all. It lingers on in a state of mutual hostility. If this is so, the atmosphere of tension between husband and wife can become very distressing to them both. To ease the situation, they "walk away" from each other. They may do this literally by getting out of each other's presence. The most common patterns are for the wife to go back to her mother, or for the husband to go out with his men friends or stay late at the office. But in a marriage it isn't easy for two people to go on avoiding each other. So what usually happens is that they put psychological distance, instead of physical distance, between them. They do this by a kind of tacit agreement not to discuss the areas of their disagreement. This means keeping their relationship on a superficial level. The result is that a cooling process slowly takes place, and the warmth and spontaneity of their love gradually die. This is a common sequence of events in modern marriages, very familiar to marriage counselors. Sometimes the couple will go on living together for years in a state of armed truce. Sometimes the marriage slowly disintegrates, as the areas of shared living gradually wither away.

The third way is the only one that really works in a modern marriage. But it isn't easy to apply. It is called by Professor Oeser, the Australian social psychologist, the "syncratic cooperative" method. It really means settlement by negotiation; getting behind the conflict, and behind the disagreement, to the underlying differences, and trying honestly together to understand them and to see what can be done about them.

Obviously this is impossible unless the couple can communicate. And this means breaking the silence, lowering the angry tone of the voices, letting the rage and resentment subside and facing the situation with genuine willingness to see the other's point of view. This is asking a great deal of some people, and it is one of the reasons why marriage won't work unless the partners have a reasonable degree of maturity; because it takes maturity to put yourself in a position that may result in your not getting your own way, and admitting that your partner has claims that must be satisfied at your expense.

Yet unless married couples can somehow manage to resolve their conflicts by negotiation and compromise, it is a sad fact that they can never really live a shared life. So the ability to communicate effectively, and to resolve conflict creatively, is absolutely essential for the building of a good marriage.

It is this which enables a couple to encourage and support each other as they face life's inevitable challenges, to comfort and succor each other in the hour of defeat. It enables them to exercise a mutual ministry toward each other, aid each other's spiritual growth, and as someone aptly put it, "hold each other up to the highest."

In all this there is a hidden factor that can make all the difference to couples who share a religious faith. If they truly believe that they were called by God into the shared life of marriage, they have a powerful resource for dealing with conflict. For in every significant decision in their lives, they are committed not to having their own way, but to finding together the will of God. This immediately shifts the focus of the decision they have to make to a higher plane and opens up the way for the finding of an effective solution to their conflicts. It helps them, also, to be genuinely concerned about each other's needs and ready to forgive each other's shortcomings. The whole atmosphere of marriage is changed from a grim struggle for rights to a ministry of mutual support. Conflict for such people becomes a means toward deeper understanding of themselves and of each other, a means of growing together as persons and in the unity of the shared life.

6

Work and Money

•

IT WOULD BE NICE IF MARRIAGE could be what it is in our romantic dreams—two people, deeply in love, walking off together into the woods, with a carpet of spring flowers beneath their feet, birds singing, and not a care in the world!

But it is not so. Marriage is establishing a new unit of human society. That means a home, and furniture, and utilities, and a car (perhaps two), and bills, and garbage collection, and much else besides. Hard, unromantic realities—yet your marriage can't work at the emotional and spiritual levels unless the business of homemaking runs smoothly.

A few fortunate people are born with silver spoons in their mouths and inherit enough money to take them comfortably through life. But the rest of us have to earn an income by considerable expenditure of either physical or mental effort, or a combination of both. We recognize that begging bowls and other devices have secured handouts for special people in religious communities; but we believe it is in accordance with all widely accepted religious principles that the great majority of us will have to work for a living.

Our patterns have changed a good deal. Traditionally, husband and wife both worked at home, though their spheres were rather sharply divided. On the farm the husband worked outside the house, the wife inside—though there were some overlapping, as when the wife took care of the chickens, milked the cows, grew fruit and vegetables for kitchen use. When the husband was an artisan or craftsman or shopkeeper, his workshop was usually attached to the home. So the married couple were close to each other most of the time, took their meals together, and were familiar with each other's tasks. They learned to cooperate and to help each other out to some extent when the going was hard.

With the coming of an urban-industrial society this pattern changed. The husband's work moved farther and farther from his home—or perhaps we should put it the other way around! He was now away from home most of the day, leaving after breakfast and returning for the evening meal. The wife continued her homemaking tasks, but as she had access to better utensils and appliances and to prepared and packaged foods, her work burden grew lighter. This made life easier for her, but it wasn't as interesting. She felt cut off from the real activities of her world. She wanted to be "with it," to go "where the action is." She began to develop what Margaret Mead has called the "trapped housewife syndrome."

All over the world, for countless wives, World War II changed the pattern again. Married women were drafted into the labor force to take the places of their fighting men. They found themselves in the worlds of commerce, of industry, of public service, of government—hitherto almost exclusive masculine preserves. They became familiar with the environment into which their husbands had disappeared ten hours a day. They found it tough, but also exhilarating. They tasted independence and knew what it was to have money of their own to spend. They had a feeling of emancipation.

After the war, everything was supposed to "go back to normal." But in some areas this didn't happen. One was the employment of wives. Their labor couldn't be easily or quickly dispensed with. And they didn't all *want* to go back. It wasn't just that they needed the money. They had tasted freedom, and home for some of them was a gilded cage. So the "working wife" became an institution, and we began to talk about the "two-income family."

Let's look at this, first, from the wife's point of view. All wives don't want to be wage earners. Some don't want to be, but *have* to be—the money is essential to keep the family solvent. Others are glad to add to the family income, but that isn't their only reason, or their main reason, for working. They enjoy the challenge of a job. It gives them a sense of worth and fulfillment—unfortunately, the occupation "housewife" has low status in our culture. It gives them a chance to meet interesting people, to get out of the home and the neighborhood into the big world beyond.

But what about the husband? Some men take the traditional view. They see the woman's role as being exclusively in the home. They are opposed to the idea of their wives taking a job. When the man is as firm as this about it, the wife usually has to respect his wishes. If she opposes him, her action is a serious threat to the marriage. Sometimes, indeed, the husband's opposition is well founded—the reason the wife wants to work is to get away from an unhappy marriage!

Other men are more flexible. They see the value of the extra income. They recognize that this is important for their wives, and they don't want to stand in the way. So they help to work out an acceptable arrangement.

Even if the husband cooperates, however, there will be changes in their relationship. The home will be somewhat neglected. No more can the husband indulge the traditional phantasy of being welcomed home by his dutiful wife on the doorstep, complete with apron and flour on her hands, to be kissed and conducted to the dining room, there to be served an elegantly cooked meal with all the fixings, and then to sink into his favorite chair before the TV, while in the background he hears the gentle clatter of dishes being cleared away. The living will inevitably be a little less gracious; and he will be expected to lend a hand.

He will face the fact, too, that his wife can now relate to him on something like equal terms. She no longer lives a sheltered life. She goes out to face the world, day by day, as he does. She brings home a pay packet on Friday, as he does. She may earn as much as he does. We know one wife, professionally qualified, whose income is three times that of her husband!

If he is a sensitive man, he will be faced with another problem. His wife now has dual roles—she is a homemaker, and she is a wage earner. As a wage earner she puts in as many hours as he does. Is it reasonable and fair that, at home, she should carry the heavy end of the burden? If she has dual roles, can he justify his single role? Studies made in Russia and Scandinavia show that the working wife, who works as many hours as her husband outside the home, may put in as much as four extra hours a day on work *in* the home. The Russian wives said they had to take these hours out of sleep, recreation, and cultural pursuits. How long can a sensitive husband feel comfortable about his privileged position?

So far we have not mentioned the children. A home without a mother's presence can be a lonesome place. In Continental Europe they talk about "key children"—the boys and girls who wear the door key on a chain around their necks because they get home before their parents and have to let themselves in. The Russian schools don't allow children to return home until at least one parent is there to greet them.

In the early days of marriage there is no great problem. The wife can continue her job and help to put aside money for the heavy expenses of setting up a home. The problem is not serious, either, when the children are in their teens and relatively independent. Having a worldly-wise mother may even be an advantage to them at that stage.

The real problem focuses down on the period when the children are small and dependent. There is much to be said for the mother staying with them during these years, even if sacrifices have to be made. If she *must* go to work, it is very important that she find a really dependable mother substitute, or leave the small children in a well-organized day-care center. When this is done, the evidence from careful studies is that children don't suffer as much from the mother's absence as we formerly thought. Perhaps it is even the mother who is most deprived, missing the many episodes of her children's growth and development.

Whatever we may think of it, the pattern of the working wife and mother seems to be here to stay. It is undermining severely our traditional ideas about the roles of husband and wife, especially the concept of the husband as the head of the house. But if there are losses, there are also gains. The new kind of partnership between husband and wife, with sharing of the role of breadwinner and sharing of the role of homemaker, is in many cases creating a new comradeship in marriage that has some real advantages over the old pattern of the strong and sophisticated husband with his timid and dependent wife.

There are some changes in the work patterns of husbands, too, that are involving readjustments for the married pair. There are the "absentee husbands" whose work takes them away from the home for long stretches—air crews, traveling salesmen, truck drivers, and many others. We have had this problem before, and without the compensation provided by the long-distance telephone. A new problem of growing proportions, however, is the increasing mobility of our population, with one family in five moving every year. This inevitably throws the married couple into closer dependence on each other as they are cut off from relatives and familiar friends.

Now let us turn from the work of husband and wife to the main product of their work—money. Love of money has been called "the root of all evil." Someone else said it was "the passport to every place except heaven, and it can buy everything except happiness." It certainly produces plenty of problems in marriage. The United States is by far the wealthiest country in the world; yet almost every questionnaire on marriage problems that is circulated comes back with financial difficulties listed as problem number one.

What is wrong? Dr. Alphonse H. Clemens, Catholic University marriage counselor, believes that many married couples today "have lost their sense of values. The loss of the vision of Christian principles and virtues in matters economic; the predatory pressures of harmful advertising and salesmanship; the neo-pagan, materialistic example of all about them have given most couples a set of entirely false attitudes. They have become perplexed and muddled about the most obvious, common-sense facts." He goes on to say "These couples need re-education in primary, basic, common-sense facts of economic life."

What *are* the basic facts of economic life for people who believe that man cannot live by bread alone and that there is more to life than making and spending money? What are the ground rules of money management for married couples for whom religious faith is important?

We have tried to answer the question from our own personal experience. We have come up with seven rules, which we believe would represent the kind of money policy that has worked well for many couples besides ourselves.

1) *Settle for a sensible standard of living.* American life is keenly competitive, and success tends to be judged in material terms: the kind of house we live in, the kind of car we drive, the social set to which we attach ourselves. It seems to us that social climbing does not accord well with a religious view of human life, and that we should firmly resist the pressures around us to keep us with the Joneses, or even to get ahead of them!

A great many money troubles in American families stem from the anxious effort to measure up to standards of living that are incompatible with their resources. So it would be wise for a married couple to consider carefully where they can comfortably fit on the socioeconomic scale. Having done so, they should then establish their home among people who are at their own earning level, or even a little below it. This will free them and their children from the purposeless tensions that assail people who are reaching too high and finding they have to stand awkwardly on their tiptoes in order to be noticed.

As Quakers, we personally accept a standard of simplicity as being more appropriate than one of luxury, in a world where there is so much poverty and need. Also there is a tradition that plain living and high thinking go well together.

The standard accepted by a couple will decide how much work will be needed to meet it. When husbands start "moonlighting," and wives feel compelled to leave the home to earn a supplementary income, the question must always be asked, "Is this being done to provide necessities, or luxuries?"

2) *Live within your income.* In the past it was considered a disgrace to be in debt; but nowadays this has become entirely respectable, and is even enjoined as being good for the national economy. There are exceptional items that often cannot be paid for when they are needed: a house, and a car that is a necessity. There are times of crisis that cannot be anticipated when borrowing money is the only sensible thing to do. But as a general rule, we believe it is good policy for a family to pay its way and keep out of debt.

3) *Pool your resources and decide together how to use them.* Willingness to stop saying "mine" and "yours" and instead to say "ours" is a vital test of unity and mutual trust in a marriage. We have known husbands who didn't tell their wives what their income was, and wives who hid away private resources. In every case, this defensive attitude showed up plainly in other areas of the marriage. We have pleaded in an earlier chapter for honesty and openness between husband and wife; and this should certainly include the area of money management.

However, pooling resources should always be accompanied by joint decisions about how to use them. All decisions about major policy and about large and unusual expenditures should be arrived at in democratic fashion after full discussion. And we would recommend that this should normally be a *family* council, with children included in what can be for them a valuable learning experience. But, knowing how touchy discussions of family finance can be, we would offer a special caution: avoid getting into disagreements about money management late in the evening!

4) *Know where your money is going.* Even in a normal family, money matters can be quite surprisingly complicated. This can't be avoided; and the only way to deal with it is to be businesslike. This has two implications. First, husband and wife should both understand clearly what their financial situation is: how much comes in, how much goes in taxes, what the major recurring expenses are, and so on. Second, records should be kept of all expenditures—apart from purely personal items out of an agreed allowance.

If these simple tasks are carried out, discussions of the financial situation will be based on the real facts of the case. Many bitter wrangles about money management turn out to be based on misconceptions and misunderstandings. It doesn't matter who keeps the records. Some husbands feel this is their prerogative. Some wives are such good financiers that their husbands cheerfully let them take over. It might be a good idea to take turns in alternate years!

5) *Have an agreed and realistic spending policy.* The experts always favor budgets, and clearly this makes sense. Some couples get discouraged at the elaborate calculations that seem to be involved and prefer to use trial and error. Either way, what is essential is to make a regular review of what is being spent, with all the facts and figures on the table. If husband and wife are flexible, they can make minor adjustments as they go along, pulling back when the kitty is low, holding off on nonessential items until there is a balance in hand.

It is important to provide a personal allowance for every family member—husband, wife, and each child—which can be spent without consulting the others, and no questions asked. It is unfair to expect a housewife to pay for personal items from housekeeping money. Personal allowances should be reviewed from time to time in the light of experience, to see whether they are adequate in relation to the available resources. It is a valuable part of a child's upbringing that he should learn at an early age to experiment with money management, and learn the facts of life in this important area.

6) *Plan for the long-term future.* The first basic requirement here is insurance. It is the duty of every responsible married couple to face the fact that the unexpected can happen and that provision must be made for the family's economic survival if the breadwinner cannot longer function. Fortunately in these days disasters are somewhat cushioned by welfare provisions of the state. But this nearly always has to be supplemented, and a sound insurance program is essential. In the early years, when money is scarce, a couple may get by with term insurance, and then switch to ordinary life. Basic insurance covering major possessions like the house or the car is also highly desirable.

Future planning also calls for a sound savings program to cover major items which cannot be met out of regular income. In the life of the average couple there are three clearly recognizable stages that should guide their accumulation of capital. In the early years the aim should be to own their own home and equip it to meet their needs as soon as possible. Next they move to the stage of providing higher education for their children. When this has been done, they must concentrate on building economic security for their retirement years. The fact that our needs are expanding while inflation is diminishing our resources means, unfortunately, that for most couples saving will be a continuous process right up to retirement. This discipline must however be faced. It is folly to fritter money away on unimportant trifles and then be unable to cope with major economic needs.

7) *Contribute wisely to good causes.* People of religious faith regard their money as they regard life itself—as a trust to be rightly used. We call this the concept of stewardship. As God has

prospered us, we want to respond by helping the needy. So we set aside a part of what we have so that we may bestow it where, in our judgment, it will do the most good.

Some still follow the traditional practice of tithing: setting aside a tenth of all income received (before or after taxes have been deducted). Some prefer to give on a more flexible basis: smaller contributions in tight periods, larger gifts when resources are more abundant. There can be no universal rule to fit us all. We would emphasize, however, the need to give wisely. There are causes that deserve our support and causes that don't, and we have to try to distinguish between them. Money given to meet real need at the right time can work something approaching miracles. Our responsibility for almsgiving doesn't end when the money has been set aside. The real responsibility is to choose, with wisdom and imagination, the recipient of the gift.

Before we conclude this discussion of money we must add what we consider to be a very important observation. The financial problems of married couples are in most cases not financial problems at all. They are personal problems that show up in an area of the shared life that is wide open to disagreement and conflict. In our culture, money is the medium through which we project the image we have and want others to have of ourselves. It is the means by which we can best manipulate other people: impress them, buy their favor, get their attention, solicit their service. Holding on to money gives us a sense of security; spending it lavishly gives us a sense of abandon. Apart from necessities, the things we buy are the means by which we seek happiness, social status, escape, revenge—even love.

So, while it is good and wise to follow a sensible money policy, this alone will not solve our financial problems. When married people have a disagreement about money, it's good for them to ask themselves, "What is it we are *really* fighting about? What unsolved problem in our relationship does this conflict over money express?" The answer to these questions can be very revealing.

7

The Maturing of Love

•

FOR FOLLOWERS OF THE JUDEO-CHRISTIAN TRADITION the supreme vocation is to reflect in their lives the love of God. This can be done by teaching and preaching. But it is done far more convincingly by living, by action.

Marriage is a close, intimate relationship which, as we understand it today, is based on love. We would probably all agree that it reaches its highest and best when it comes nearest to expressing the love of God. When husband and wife are nearest to God, therefore, they are nearest to the achievement of a perfect marriage.

The maturing of love in a human relationship is a long, slow process that takes a lifetime. Love has many aspects and many phases. The English language, rich in many respects, is seriously deficient in having only one little word to cover so much variety. The Greeks were better off. They had at least three words for love, and these can help us to understand the complexity of the relationship of husband and wife.

First there is the word *eros,* which can be interpreted in many ways. It usually represents for us the love that is *desire*—the desire of the man for the woman and of the woman for the man. We generally think of this as *sexual* desire; and the word "erotic" certainly has this meaning. But a man can desire a woman in other ways too; he can see her as enhancing his ego, as being useful to him in his social life and his career. And we shouldn't think of *eros* as a low and unworthy form of love. There is desire in all love—even the love of God for man. So desire is a proper element in love. But alone it is not true love, and has no power to endure. For if love is only desire, then when desire dies down, love vanishes.

The second Greek word is *philia*, which means friendship-love. It inspired the name Philadelphia, the city of "brotherly love." This is nonsexual love, the kind that is felt by people who have much in common, who see life in the same way, who enjoy each other's company. This is quite important in mariage, as we shall see later.

The third Greek word is *agape* (pronounced ah-gah-pay) which was a word taken over by the early Christian Church and given a special meaning. It is what we mean when we speak of "altruism": a disinterested concern for others, a *devotion* for a loved person which asks for nothing in return. This is the caring kind of love, the serving and sacrificing kind, which is described in the words of Jesus, "Greater love hath no man than this, that a man lay down his life for his friends." It is based not on blind devotion, but on appreciation of the true *worth* of the other person. In this connection it is helpful to remember that our English word "worship" really means "worth-ship"—devotion given to a person as a recognition of his worth.

These ideas begin to show us how many facets there are in love. If marriage is to work, it needs all three. Desire brings the couple together in the first place and continues to hold them to one another. Friendship builds harmony and mutual understanding between them. Devotion carries them over the rough spots and keeps them loyal and faithful to each other.

What part in all this does *romantic love* play? In our modern world, romance has been given great importance. A cult of romance was begun in medieval Europe; but we don't agree with the people who suggest it was unknown before that time. Some of the oldest poems in the world, the Chinese odes of the fifth century B.C., are very romantic.

Freud said that love was "aim-inhibited sex," and this gives us a significant clue. When two people feel sex attraction for each other but hold back their sexual desire for some reason, this generates a state of emotional yearning that is the basis of romance. In its early adolescent form it is called "infatuation." But it matures late and gains considerable refinement. The state of being in love is a very delightful one, though often disturbing as well. It provides a fine start for a marriage, like the rocket that soars into the air and puts the space capsule in orbit. But like the rocket, its intensity is so great that it soon burns itself out. Sexual fulfillment to the point of familiarity and routine brings it to an end. It cannot possibly last long in a marriage, and a marriage based only on romantic love has no power to endure.

Bishop Fulton J. Sheen, in a press interview, once made this point when he said, "This is the story of virtually every marriage. Once the passion subsides, the marriage declines." And Thornton Wilder, in his book *The Bridge of San Luis Rey*, says of one of his characters: "She had never realized any love save love as passion. Such love, though it expends itself in generosity and thoughtfulness, though it give birth to visions and to great poetry remains among the sharpest expressions of self-interest. Not until it has passed through a long servitude, through its own self-hatred, through mockery, through great doubts, can it take its place among the loyalties. Many who have spent a lifetime in it can tell us less of love than the child that lost a dog yesterday."

What must happen is that romantic love, before it dies away, must be replaced by what we call *conjugal love*. This is a quieter and less exciting attachment between a man and a woman, but it is more durable. We will return to this later.

When we speak of sexual love, we should remember that sex and love are not the same, though we often talk about them loosely as if they were. You can have sex without love, and you can have love without sex. One of the greatest achievements of human culture is to bring them together and bind them into one.

The Christian tradition made a sad mistake when it took the view that the only purpose of sex was procreation. This is its obvious *biological* purpose. But as Sherwin Bailey has made very clear, the Bible recognizes *two* distinct purposes of sex: the *procreative* end, which is biological, and the *unitive* end, which is relational. Sex not only makes it possible for husband and wife to have children. It also, as a recurring need, brings them back again and again to a renewal of their unity; and their unity and emotional harmony provide the right emotional atmosphere for the healthy development of the children born to them.

So the sex life of the married couple is not a part of their life to be ashamed of. It is a God-given experience of delight in each other. Christians see in it a sacramental quality. A sacrament is defined as "the outward and visible sign of an inward and spiritual grace." And that exactly describes the sexual union of a happily married couple. Their physical union symbolizes and renews their love for one another. It is not in itself a part of love; but it becomes the supreme expression of love between husband and wife.

People sometimes speak of sex as good or beautiful. Their intentions are excellent, but they are mistaken. Sex in itself is simply a part of life—life, indeed, as God planned. But whether sex in any given situation is good or bad, beautiful or ugly, depends entirely on the way it is used. Love and lust are completely opposite: one gives, the other takes; one serves, the other exploits. Yet the sexual act which expresses both is exactly the same. It is the feelings, the intentions, and the attitudes of the people involved that make the difference.

What we do in marriage, therefore, is to take sexual desire, which need have nothing to do with love, and make it the expression of married love. As we develop the shared life of marriage, we use sexual intercourse to express the closeness we feel to each other, and to give each other comfort and fulfillment. But the sex life of the couple cannot by itself sustain married love.

This is a very common illusion. It is the other way round—married love must sustain the sex life.

A great deal is being written today about sexual technique. It is good that we are learning about such things. But there is a great danger that we should become so preoccupied with techniques and orgasms that we put the cart before the horse. Many people today think of sexual intercourse as a *performance*—a manipulation of each other's bodies to bring about the correct result. We certainly need to understand the ways in which our bodies function. But sexual intercourse, to be humanly satisfying, must be an *experience* shared by two persons. It is possible to "go through the motions" perfectly correctly and yet to miss the "experience." As one wife put it rather pointedly, "We don't have sexual intercourse any more. You see, there is nothing left for it to express."

Once we have shifted the emphasis from performance to experience, we are set free from questions about what positions to adopt, how often is correct, and so on. If we make the sex life of the couple a grimly serious business, it may ultimately fail to function altogether. If we put the emphasis on making it an experience of mutual joy and happiness, however it is done, each couple will find the pattern that suits them best.

So we come back again to the love of the couple for each other, and the growth of this conjugal love. Unfortunately we can't assume that love naturally matures in marriage. It doesn't. The studies that have been made suggest that, as the years pass, most couples tend to be increasingly disenchanted with their marriages. So married love seems to be like a garden. Cultivated, it becomes a source of great delight. Neglected, it soon deteriorates.

Our experience of marriage, our own and other people's, has convinced us that what makes a marriage endure and grow is not sex attraction or romantic love, as many imagine, but the cultivation of the shared life. An English bishop some years ago, in a press interview, said that marriage was just a lifelong friendship between a man and a woman, with a dash of sex thrown in. He was much criticized for this very prosaic and unromantic definition. But we are convinced that he was right. If two married people can learn to understand and comfort and support and help each other through all the changing experiences of human life, everything else will fall into place. But it takes conscious effort to do this; and sustained effort. Marriage is, in fact, for religious people, a vocation.

Each successive stage of married life brings its own special challenges and opportunities. The love of the early years is exuberant. It is based on the joy and delight of belonging completely to one another, the excitement of new experiences, the comfort and reassurance of being loved and cherished. But soon the couple become more and more deeply involved in responsibilities. The children come along and consume the young wife's time and energy. The husband meanwhile is preoccupied with his career, striving to equip himself to attain his economic goals. Unless they make time to keep in real communication with each other, the marriage during these strenuous years may begin to wither for lack of nourishment. But if they resolutely support and help each other, this can be a time when their comradeship gains greatly in depth and strength.

As the couple move into what we call the early middle years, the tensions ease a little. The children learn to stand on their own feet and need less attention. The husband finds his level in the business world and, if he is a sensible man, settles down to a less strenuous pace. This can be a time of more gracious living, with some leisure to enjoy life together. But it can also be "the dangerous forties," bringing anxiety and insecurity to the wife as she recognizes that her children no longer need her, and as the menopause and the beginning of the aging process remind her physically she has passed her peak. The husband may at this time go through a period of disillusionment as he faces the hard fact that his ambitions will not be fulfilled and he will have to settle for less than he hoped for. A loving couple can sustain each other through these difficult adjustments; but if they have not stayed close together, they may take out their fears and frustrations on each other and drift further apart.

The later middle years come all too soon. Now the pace *must* slacken, as energy levels fall. But yet these can be the happiest years of all. The nest is empty, and they are free to relax on the porch or widen their horizons by travel. They are on a pleasant plateau, with no more mountains to climb. They have given up sighing for what is beyond their reach and have settled for life as it is. If through the years they have kept their marriage in good repair, love at this time will be mellow and mature. Husband and wife enjoy a comfortable acceptance of one another, giving each other the comfort and companionship that they increasingly need.

So the couple move together into the later years and retirement. Now the comradeship they have built up through a lifetime together comes to full fruition. As their physical powers diminish, they lean on each other more and more for support. Now they become spectators, and no longer participants in the drama of human history. This is the time for evaluation, for the sharing of memories, for the leisurely cultivation of common interests and common friends, for the perfecting of faith and love.

Felix Adler, the Jewish philosopher, has described the closing years of a good marriage so well that we conclude this chapter with his words:

> Together they have traveled the road of life, and remembrance now holds them close, remembrance of many hours of ineffable felicity, of a sense of union as near to bliss as mortal hearts can realize, of sorrow shared—sacramental sorrows. And now, nearing the end, hand in hand they look forth upon the wide universe, and the love which they found in themselves, and still find there to the last, becomes to them the pledge of a vaster love that moves beyond the stars and the suns.

PART III

●

WHEN YOU BECOME
PARENTS

8

Your Love's Incarnation: Your Children

•

HAROLD J. BELGUM

Harold J. Belgum is Secretary for Family Life Education for the Board of Parish Education of the American Lutheran Church, in Minneapolis, Minnesota. Because he was trained in social work, his writings and artistic creations articulate his deep concerns for the "povertied" (his term for those who have been ground down by poverty) of all races and nations. He inspired the founding of the Interfaith Commission on Marriage and Family Life, on which he served as a charter member, and he has been responsible for creating inter-faith and inter-professional dialogues to promote interest in families. He is married and the father of three.

•

No HUMAN ENTERPRISE IS SO COMPLEX or so awesome as family life. Nowhere else in our society are two persons asked to carry such heavy responsibilities. A father and a mother are expected to create children, to build into them a moral and spiritual and civic conscience, to bring them into responsible adulthood without delinquency or disaster.

Millions of couples are engaged in this "impossible enterprise." We are not alone! Let us make common cause with those who are in the same stage of family life as we are. If we have just had our first child, let's find others who have just had their first child. If our oldest is entering first grade, let's find other parents whose oldest is new in this same experience. If we have a son or daughter just coming into seventh grade, let's find other families who are in the same dilemma.

Our children are our first and greatest concern. We set out to find other parents whose children are in the same stage of growth as our own. We phone them. We go to visit them. We invite them over. We meet them at the PTA. We seek them out. Our schools are a common ground for the interfaith, intercultural, and intersocial meeting with parents *truly concerned about their children*. School learnings are footnotes to the work of the Creator of heaven and earth. Take very seriously what your child brings home from school and relate it to your religious beliefs. As you meet other parents with children in the same grade you can get clues to the nature of man and the purpose of the Creator.

WHAT IS A FAMILY FOR?

A generation ago few would have asked this question. Today many do. I consider this a religious question. I believe the family is an important aspect of the Creator's design for human life and society. The shape and style of family life have changed enormously. However, no satisfactory substitutes have been found for certain functions of the family. In spite of social change and mobility and urban crises and a revolution every month somewhere in the world, it still seems to me that the following functions are best carried out inside a family, hopefully with father and mother still living:

1) *The family is the best place to make babies and to take care of them.* Making babies is the easiest thing in the world. But taking good care of them isn't so easy. Anyone who has seen the movies Dr. Spitz made of babies that had been alone in their cribs for a year, cared for impersonally, will never forget it. These babies just stared ahead or rocked to and fro and didn't respond even to friendly persons. They belonged to a vegetable kingdom.

They hadn't had mothering, tender loving and fun-filled care and play.

2) *The family is the best place to get the feeling that you belong.* When your parents take care of you because they care about you, then you begin sensing what it means to belong. You belong to them. They belong to you. They belong to each other. This feeling gives a deep and enduring satisfaction. There is much emotion and unconscious meaning in it. It has to do with self-worth, value, usefulness, goodness, and love. Persons who feel valueless are dangerous. Dr. Bowlby found that good maternal care of young children is the best insurance for good mental health when they grow up.

3) *The family is the best place to form a conscience.* Conscience is a big word. It has to do with good and evil, blessings and curses, helping and hurting. Conscience is what makes it possible for people to live together in peace and harmony and cooperation. Children build their own consciences by watching their parents and other "big" people. Some people we call "psychopaths." They have no clear sense of good and evil. When they were children they were unable to form a conscience. They have flimsy guide lines for conduct. They respect neither people nor property. They live confused lives. Children need to develop a sense of responsibility as men and women of tomorrow. How to become a man or a woman, a good and real person, is best learned at home.

4) *The family is the best place to develop good habits.* We call habits good or bad depending on whether they help us get more out of life or deprive us of certain benefits of life. Habits have their effect on ourselves and on others. Habits have to do with our use of money, for instance: wasteful habits, saving habits, useful habits. Shirking responsibility is a habit learned in the family. Carrying your fair share is a habit learned in the family. Habits of order or disorder, responsibility or irresponsibility are picked up in the family. "As the twig is bent the tree will grow."

5) *The family is the best place to get interested in the world.* When a child hears his mother on the phone saying, "Well, if you have to go to see your doctor this afternoon, Gregg and Sylvia can come over to our house and play with Erik and Rolf." The world widens. It begins to include a neighbor family whose mother is sick. Or Father reads out loud from the evening paper, "Floods threaten three cities. Help needed for families whose homes are destroyed." Then if Father gets out his checkbook and sends money to help, the children are turned from selfishness toward helpfulness and citizenship. The family is the incubator of statesmen.

POTENTIALS OF FAMILY LIFE

If you agree in the main that these *five functions* are best carried out in a normal family, then let's look at the family from another point of view. These five functions are minimal. What is "ideal"? What is the best and fullest expression of family life? I guess I'd call these "potentials of family life" or "wonderful possibilities."

1) A good family lets each child unfold in his or her own peculiar and unique way. Granted, you can't let them wreck your best dishes just because they are outgoing. But within reasonable limits of safety and sanitation, you can let them be themselves, "do their thing." That's a great gift in this day of standardized expectations and monotonous routine.

2) A good family takes seriously the physical necessities: food, shelter, clothing, safety, health. After all, the children's bodies are basic. Immunization against disease is as important as a good conscience. If you're dead, your well-developed conscience can't do any good.

3) A good family passes on to the children a cluster of values: religious, political, social, civic—yes, economic too. Parents give their children a sense of some kind of "ladder of values." All good

things aren't on the same level. Some experiences are *much more* important than others. Things . . . ideas . . . persons. . . .

4) A good family sets goals. The parents decide to do things and if humanly possible they do them. If they make promises, they keep them. They help their children aim for certain objectives and work to attain them. They don't approve of "copping out." They give their children reasonable responsibilities and hold them to the assignments as best they can.

5) A good family will have general rules that apply to all members. Parents will be flexible and allow a good deal of give and take but they will agree on certain "do's" and "don't's." Just as a country needs laws, so does a family. If you think a law is unfair in a certain instance, you can "take it to court."

6) A good family allows the father to be a man and go out and mix with men, the mother to go out and mix with women. Married couples need to maintain good connections with their own sex. Then too a good family respects the rights of Mom and Dad to have their own times together. A friend of mine has a rule that when he gets home from work, he and his wife have a half hour of private conversation; children respect this. Then there are family times too.

7) A good family has fun and fellowship and warmth and games and jokes—all together. This isn't easy to manage if there are wide age differences but the *intention is there*. So fighting begins. So what? Life is full of fights. The big thing is to intend to have a good time that includes everyone. Hang in there!

8) A good family has a certain flexibility and adaptability and bounce. Then if certain planned good times don't come off, not everyone feels so guilty. If a kid does a bad thing, the whole family doesn't go to pieces. They may give him "what for," but he's still *in the family* as solidly as if he'd done a good thing. Some people call it forgiveness, others acceptance.

9) A good family is "all ears." When someone has something

to say or is in a fix, the others try to listen and to understand. They don't preach until they've heard the problem or the question. If someone wants to be alone, they don't bug him. They let him be till he's ready to talk. They think privacy is important.

10) A good family is where much of the teaching and preaching is nonverbal. The children absorb it through simply watching how their parents live and act. One act is worth a thousand words. If parents show self-control under stress, the kids absorb it. If parents are generous to needful neighbors, the kids learn to be.

11) A good family helps other families. No matter how complex and busy the family life becomes, let there happen a tragedy or an emergency in the neighborhood—the busyness will stop and larger duties will be seen. Even at a hint of trouble, a good family will show tactful concern and offer to help.

12) A good family is political. This simply means that in addition to helping the family three doors down who had a fire in their house, the family (led of course by the parents) keep alive the idea that a major way to help other families is through political action. Children learn this in school. Reinforce it at home!

9

Infancy and Early Childhood

●

THE ARRIVAL OF A NEW HUMAN BEING on this pitiful planet is as majestic a moment as the arrival of Christopher Columbus on San Salvador. The newborn baby is as complex and as full of unknown potential as the continent of Africa. But more intriguing than either the majesty or the complexity of your baby's being is the fact that your baby is an "act of God." By this I mean that in your baby you can see the intentions He has for all mankind. Your child was born in the image of God.

THE IMAGE OF GOD

What does this mean to you? To find the answer you will have to observe your baby as he (or she) grows and grows and grows. Part of my religious faith is this: "The Most Unusual Person" who created everyone had in mind a certain pattern for human beings. We all have nine systems:

1) *Bone*—206 different bones forming the framework of life.
2) *Muscular*—600 and more muscles move body and organs to make life a moving affair.
3) *Nervous*—A complex network like radio, telephone, and television to connect us with each other.
4) *Digestive*—Sorts out foods and drinks and converts them to energy to give us power.

5) *Respiratory*—Takes oxygen from the air; sends out carbon dioxide.
6) *Circulatory*—Sends blood to the tiniest capillaries.
7) *Lymphatic*—A colorless and valuable fluid which bathes and feeds every cell of the body.
8) *Endocrine*—These glands are regulators of all systems. They send out signals that tell how fast each system is to grow and develop.
9) *Reproductive*—Here is a radical division depending on whether your baby is a male or female. This system contains the power to reproduce human beings. Each human being reproduced will have all nine systems described.

Footnote on Sex Education: The way father and mother act toward each other is the most important ingredient of sex education for young children. This gives them their clues as to the complementarity of male and female. This gives boys their ideas of chivalry and the girls their ideas of femininity.

What I am suggesting is that "sex education" is best woven into the whole fabric of growth. It is certainly a frank recognition of physical differences. But it is also much more: the complementarity of male and female, the high soprano voice and the basso profundo, the rocking of a baby to a lullaby and the riveting of a great bridge to span a river.

Sex education begins at birth. It is caught rather than taught. Certainly factual information is needed, but the emotional environment that receives it is of supreme importance. This is formed early in life.

ENJOY YOUR BABY'S GROWTH!

Four ways to observe what is happening:

1) *The marvelous development of the body:* the intricate relationship between the mouth, the eyes, the hands. The mouth

is so important. Sucking gives nourishment and comfort. Soon it is used for testing and tasting new things. The eyes and the neck muscles seem to work together. Soon the baby is turning his head to watch you. Then he finds his hands and suspects they are very important. He studies them. Before you know it, he grabs a dish and smash it goes on the floor. Before long he sits alone . . . then he crawls . . . then he walks . . . then he runs . . . then he's on his tricycle . . . watch out for the cars. . . . He's three years old!

2) *The magic of mind over matter:* The baby's mastery of the world of things proceeds as swiftly as his physical development. He notes new sounds, recognizes a lullaby, feels strange in a strange place, reacts to a new smell, pokes with his fingers, bangs things to see what happens. He discovers and explores. He looks behind things. He kicks, pushes, and climbs to see over things. He experiments. This is how he begins his learning life. He pretends he is a cat. He crawls and "meows" under the table. He looks for missing toys. All the time you know his mental life is growing at the same rapid pace that his body is maturing.

3) *The wonder of words:* Every sound your baby hears or makes is practice and preparation for the art of language. Watch how language begins: he listens intently, buzzes with lips, tries out different levels of pitch, makes faces along with certain sounds, gestures with other sounds, responds to his name. By the time he is three years old he may well know a thousand words. How did he learn them? By listening and by making sounds and by connecting them with meanings. But words are only one kind of language. There are languages of behavior, of mood, of climate— and these languages have much to do with relationships to persons. Words are for expression of self and relationship with others.

4) *The mystery of human relationships:* Really, the growth of the body, the development of the mind, and the learning of language all come together in the baby's relationship with persons —in the family and outside. We are created for others. From the

beginning, you noted your baby's sense of society. He liked to be picked up, rocked, sung to, played with. His first laugh was a milestone in social formation. When he got you to laugh, it was another. When he first "did a job," when he first decided to "go potty in the pot," he made a leap toward civilized society—which is really relationship.

THE GATES OF GOD

What gives enjoyment to babies and young children? Eminently their five senses. St. Augustine called the five senses "the Gates of God." Through these gates come an unbelievable array of experiences:

Good tastes (candy, gum, and what not)
Good smells (my soap, Mother's perfume, Dad's shaving lotion, etc.)
Good sounds (music, lullabies, friendly greetings, et al.)
Good feelings (bath, holdings, warm bed, etc.)
Good sights (colors galore, flowers, clothes with patterns, pleasant faces, pets, etc.).

For children it is like the dawn of creation when God looked out and said, "Behold, it is all very good." At this moment we won't bother about the snake and the devil and the fall and original sin—we'll just say that for little children there is a grand amount of enjoyment available through their five senses and they deserve it. If you and your marriage mate feel life is very good, then your children will catch the idea.

Humor and fun are essential in your roles as parents. Humor and comedy have to do with the difference between your plans and your performance. They have to do with your ability to laugh at yourself—and to laugh *with* others, *not at them,* when they take a pratfall.

THE PLOT THICKENS

As your children grow there are four great assets you, as parents, can give them.

1) *Self-confidence.* If you've never read Emerson's Essay on "Self-Reliance," now is a good time to read it. How does trust grow in a child? I suppose he has *to be trusted.* I suppose he has to feel that his parents trust each other and somehow trust the Creator who made us all come alive.

2) *Civilization.* Self-control begins with the mastery of the basic human needs to urinate and to excrete in certain places at certain times. If the child learns to handle these needs in a way that is OK with other people, he is on his way to membership in civilized society. Then he can move on to manners and to etiquette.

3) *Nerve.* Many people talk about a "failure of nerve" in American society. It's another way of saying "initiative"—the ability to come forward, to stand up for what you believe, to go out and try to get what you want—whether it is a mate or a job or another kind of honor or satisfaction. Protect your pre-schoolers from those who try in many ways to cut the nerve of their initiative. Help them to be true, if little, persons.

4) *Conscience.* The ability to discriminate between what helps others and what hurts others. The idea of "the righteous man." The idea of "the good citizen." The whole question of a nation's morality and a society's ethics is determined before the future citizens enter first grade. The inner core of the personality is formed at home, in the family. The conscience of the child is the governor of the upcoming society.

MORE ABOUT "THE IMAGE OF GOD"

I'm sure you suspect I was kidding when I suggested that the "Image of God" meant 200 bones and 600 muscles, etc., etc. In a way I was, but still I wanted to get you to consider that the physical shape we have represents some kind of perfection in creation. For instance, try to think of other physical arrangements for making babies and see what they would lead to. Try to think about the advantages of having three eyes or five ears. But there are other and more intriguing aspects of the Image of God . . . for instance:

1) It is somehow Godlike to prefer order to chaos, use to abuse, cleanliness to filth, beauty to ugliness, shapeliness to monstrosity. Your pre-school child somehow has these preferences.

2) It is somehow Godlike to prefer good over evil, kindness over cruelty, regularity and rhythm over irregularity, unpredictability and sheer noise. Your pre-schooler fears violence and prefers peace.

3) It is somehow Godlike to come close to other people. To listen to them. To help them. To bring them forward. To encourage them. To lift them up if they fall. This appeals to your pre-schooler. He may enjoy pushing someone down—but even more he enjoys helping someone up. If he helps someone he doesn't like, he's especially proud.

10

Your Firstborn Leads the Way

•

LONG AGO PRIMOGENITURE WAS AN IMPORTANT LAW. This law gave
to the firstborn child certain privileges that could not be taken
away. Even today in royal families the firstborn child succeeds to
the throne. To our democratic way of thinking, this special status
for the firstborn goes against the grain. We want equality. We
want no inborn differences. We want an aristocracy of merit.
Everyone starts on an equal footing.

But family life isn't that way. One child simply must be born
first. No matter how many come after, the firstborn boy or girl
is always the oldest—the first to begin school, the first to graduate,
the first to enter the world as an independent human being.

I think it's very important for parents to accept this fact that
"firstborn" is first. Like Washington! First in war, first in peace,
and first in the hearts of his countrymen. "Last-born" is unique too,
often treated as the baby of the family even into adulthood.
"Last-born" has a uniqueness all his own. "Middle-born" is unique
too. He is born into a squeeze play. Each child is unique. His
particular position in the family is determined by the number of
children older than he and younger than he. Actually, each
child is born into a different family. With each child born, the
family has grown—has changed—has expanded. As in an expanding
constellation each body moves with ever varying relations with
all the other bodies.

But the firstborn child is special in many ways. Here is the first
evidence that the husband is able to be a father. Here is the first

evidence that the wife is able to bring forth a child. No couple married can be sure they will be parents until the first child is conceived, grows month after month and finally comes out breathing. I remember when we were expecting a fifth child. We had four girls. Well-wishers pestered me with, "I'll bet you want a boy, don't you?" Once I answered abruptly, "No, all I want is a normal baby with four feet."

If we say that "family" means a father, a mother, and children, then firstborn marks the begining of your family life. The age of your family is simply the age of your firstborn child. This is one way of saying firstborn is special. He is your navigator.

When your firstborn goes out to play with other kids at the age of three, you follow him nervously to see if he'll be able to hold his own. Is he OK? Is he able to play with others or does he stand off by himself? Is he having fun? Do the other kids like him? All your own unconscious memories come alive . . . times when you were included . . . times when you were excluded. Whatever happens to him in a way happens to both of you.

FIRSTBORN SALLIES FORTH

Now it's time for first grade. Your firstborn sallies forth to learn about the great, wide, wonderful world. Now father and mother must get out of the way because Mrs. Matacheck, the first-grade teacher, is in charge of firstborn. Maybe she's too strict. Maybe she's not careful of his feelings. Maybe she draws sad faces on his work sheets when they're wrong. Firstborn is caught up in the great world of school learning and he'll get through first grade eventually. Somehow you're in first grade yourselves.

Let's switch and imagine your firstborn is a girl. Now she's in fourth grade. She's a typical politician. She gets her little friends into the yard and calls out orders. If they don't obey, she thinks of some other way to win them over. She says, "We'll have a club" . . . "We'll meet every Tuesday in our basement" . . .

"Everyone bring a candy bar." Suddenly you wonder: do I try to influence people that much? Where did she learn that stuff—from me? From my spouse? How did she get so brash? So bossy?

Before you know it she's in seventh grade—junior high. You wonder when she's going to menstruate. You're all ready to tell her when she asks. But one day it happens. Suddenly you remember the day it happened to you without warning. Then you wonder: Will I ever catch up with her and capture her attention for serious discussions about sex and womanhood? But your daughter is in her room and playing very loudly on her phonograph, "Love is something if you give it away." You listen to the words. Her door is closed. You wonder: When will be a good time to talk about it?

Let's switch again and imagine that your firstborn is a boy and now he's in tenth grade. He's entering senior high. You know he's been having wet dreams and you know (because you remember your own youth) that he is having fantastic daydreams about the mystery of girls and that most likely (as you did at his age) he is masturbating and trying to make this a genuine masculine experience. He hopes and is anxious to be a real man, find a wife, become and be a father. These are the great issues to discuss with him, not so much his present behavior. He may well feel guilty about masturbating, and you can casually let him know that it really can't harm his manhood. But talk doesn't seem to capture his imagination as much as actions and things and power and speed. You work and you wonder.

Now your firstborn daughter or son is sitting there in the senior high school graduating class. You can't believe it. It is spring. This fall he or she will be going away: to military service, to college, to a job away from home, to get married. All the new experiences of your life suddenly come to mind. Your firstborn again forces you to relive your own graduation from high school and whatever came after it. Let's imagine your firstborn has found a possible mate. Can you believe it? A different nationality? . . .

a different faith? . . . a different culture? . . . a different color? What will you do? Your veto power has expired. You'll have to rely on the controls and values that have grown inside your first-born—not much on those outside him.

Perhaps you could turn to some very basic and religious ideas:

1) All human beings are made in the image of God. This means that they all have some preference for order over disorder. This means that they have a desire to do good and restrain evil.

2) All human beings have some capacity for identifying with other human beings. That is, they have some ability to accept others different from themselves, to love them as whole persons and to help them.

3) All human beings have a *desire* to be in fellowship . . . in larger harmonious groups, groups where the true mutuality of everyone's needs are recognized.

If we truly believe these things, then we can more easily allow our firstborn son or daughter to pass beyond our family circle and determine their own lives. We can love them and let them go. And when our sons or daughters in turn bring home their first-born children, we can rejoice and be glad because this is new evidence that God the Father Almighty is still in control of his world and is bringing forth new life to replenish the earth with potential and hope.

THE SIBLING NETWORK

Let's try to put down some commonsense reminders about the "Sibling Network." For instance, what are the feelings of first-born when second-born is expected? I recall a five-year-old girl drawing this picture: She and her mother were in the lake. The mother was standing waist deep in the water. The girl drew herself at the bottom of the lake. "You can't see me," she said. "Look," said her mother, "I'm walking toward you. Then I'll feel you're there." "No," said the daughter, "you'll *just* miss me." I suppose no adult can imagine the feelings of a child who sees a little brother or sister suddenly getting a lion's share of attention. We fool ourselves if we think that somehow we can make sibling relations all loving. We speak of ambivalence, "feeling two ways at once": e.g., loving and hating. A new arrival means much sharing. We're all self-centered. It's a rough time for kids.

A four-year-old girl stood smiling down at her baby sister, and I heard her whisper, "Nice little Julie, like to get all your fingers cut off?" Karl, three years, was saying good night to the family. His new brother, Kurt, was just home from the hospital. "Good night, Mom!" "Good night, Dad!" "Good-bye, Kurt!"

My brother, Joe, was five years younger than I. He had a doll, Paul, who could summon armies of small people to defend his honor and status. Sometimes I would inquire where these small people were standing. Trustingly he would point them out. Like a fiend, I would jump up and down on them. Joe would cry, grab his doll, and run into the woods. I remember feeling half glad and half bad.

A family contains all the potentials of cooperation and helping mixed in with all the potentials for competition and hurting that can be found in a nation or in a city. There are powerful constructive and creative forces at work. Mutual concern, the sense of belonging to each other, the sense of loyalty to great ideals of faith or tradition, the experience of having Father provide and Mother prepare meals—a hundred creative and beneficent acts, words, and gestures during the day. These help overcome and modify and chanel sibling rivalries toward more interesting and more useful projects and purposes. I suppose the most important relationship of all is that between the father and the mother. This becomes a norm or model for all other relationships the children develop. If Mother and Father hang in there together, so can the children.

HOW BIG A SIBLING NETWORK?

Theodore Roosevelt invited families with twelve or more children to send him their family pictures. He would send them in return a kind of Presidential accolade for helping populate the prairies and conquer the frontier. Both my father and mother grew up in large families. They lived on the land. They were farmers.

I feel a bit uneasy discussing with you the matter of family size because you may be approaching a Theodore Roosevelt "ideal family" already. But if you are in the earlier stages of family life, or if you are just married, then here are some things worth thinking about:

If you hold to a belief in a Creator who gives to his creatures not only creative power but reason and will and conscience, then it seems all these abilities are needed to help you design the size of your sibling network. How big a network of children can you in good conscience undertake to raise, feed, clothe, house, and *bring to fulfillment of life*? It seems cruel to bring to earth human beings unless there is a fair chance for them to "explicate" themselves. I like that word. It means "unfold." Within each baby is "enfolded" unlimited possibilities. But they will not be unfolded unless there is room enough and time enough and love enough and money enough to go around.

I would rather think of "responsible parenthood" than of "birth control." The former is affirmative, the latter is negative in its connotations. There is no need here to examine the many ways in which husbands and wives can plan the dimensions and the complexity of their sibling network. Medical and psychological helps are available on every hand. Rather I would have you think about the great purposes you hold in common as a married couple, the limitations that you are willing to admit to each other and the fearless use of your reason, conscience, and will.

11

Your Family Goes to School

•

WE HAVE IMAGINED OURSELVES moving swiftly through the whole family life cycle with our firstborn child as navigator. He went ahead of us scouting the new territory. As we entered it, we found it was strangely familiar. We had been there before *at his precise age*.

TRY TO RECALL

Would you consider backtracking and moving now more slowly and thoughtfully over a six-year stretch of experience called elementary school—grades one through six? Before we begin, will you try to recall episodes from those years? Were you somewhat fearful at the very beginning? I was petrified. My mother dressed me in a beautiful blue velvet suit and white shirt and black shiny shoes. I arrived at District 78, a country schoolhouse of some thirty pupils, to find all the other boys in overalls, blue work shirts, and shoes that carried marks of the cow barn. (I'm trying to get you to remember a time you felt different, didn't fit in, didn't belong.)

Throughout the forenoon I felt sharply my strangeness, but at noon the bottom fell out. The farm kids hooted and hollered, "Lookit the Minister's kid" . . . "Look at the *Little Minister*." Suddenly what had been a pride and joy and comfort in my preschool years (my dad was a minister, he helped people meet God; family life in the parsonage had been peacefully secure)—suddenly all these great and good things seemed to be turned inside out—upside down.

Or can you possibly remember a time when you did your very best, but someone else did better—and it hurt? I don't recall the grade I was in when the multiplication tables got on the agenda, but I clearly remember how desperately I tried to memorize them. (Numbers didn't come easy for me. In college I petitioned to get out of trigonometry and was allowed to outline a "History of Mathematics"! In graduate school I came near to flunking statistics.) Day after day the teacher called out, "Stand, Pass, Sit! Recite the 'tables of 7.'" When I got up to the dizzy heights of 7×9, I'd falter. But Orlean Holten rattled them off perfectly. Day after day he outdid me in the multiplication tables. Orlean would rub salt in my wounds by observing, "Maybe you're the minister's son, but you can't beat me at *the tables*." Learning to accept defeat is a hard lesson, but it must be learned. Help your kids face it—they can't be best at everything. Everyone is "dumb" in something or in some way.

THE SIX-YEAR MARCH

From the time your firstborn marches into first grade till your last-born marches out of sixth grade and into junior high, you can for good and solid reasons consider yourselves an "elementary family." Elementary education consists of those great elements or building blocks out of which all future life is built. Don't think of "elementary" as primitive or childish—think of it as fundamental and foundational, like the elements out of which all chemical compounds are constructed.

Now if you have one child it is one kind of experience; if you have eight, as a friend of mine has, it is certainly a different kind of experience—this six-year march. But whether you have one child or eight the great issue is: Are you parents somehow marching along with your chlidren in these years when they are assembling the elements of life? Please consider the following "titles" suggestive rather than definitive. Take them seriously or humorously, whichever best fits your mood.

The First-Grader Discovers. He discovers new land as Columbus did. New buildings, new smells, new people, new rules. Most of all he discovers he is a unique and different person. This sense of newness is an exhilarating experience. It can also be devastating and depressing. It depends on the climate. Does he find friends or not? Does he meet a friendly teacher or not? As he feels his way into first grade, he discovers his ability to grow and adapt and learn. And this is fun! Enter into his excitement.

The Second-Grader Explores. Having discovered many new things in first grade, he proceeds to explore them in second grade. He will explore the meanings of words, the effect on the family of long words . . . dirty words . . . surprising words. He may begin finding models for himself which are quite different from Father and Mother. Parents should be interested and listen. But parents should also converse with the second-grader and listen to what's important to him. Probably quite important will be certain friends he's found. How do you make friends? How are you friendly? How do you erase mistakes? How do manners fit in? This can be good table talk at home.

The Third-Grader Adventures. Accidents are high for this grade, because our voyagers have become brave and want the sense of danger and risk. This is the last chance for original creativity. Next year the class and the teacher will begin to frown on originality. The third-grader begins to wonder about values. What's important and what's not? What's valuable and what's not? These are questions running through his mind. Bring him into family discussions: "Where shall we go for a weekend?" "Which of several things shall we buy?" Money gets to be important now. Money is what you use to get things and to go places and to do things. Connect this with his numbers learning in school. With his knowledge of numbers and money he can begin to be more creative. He can secure raw materials and make things rather than go out and buy ready-made "creations" to dawdle over and get bored with. Show him you too like to create—food, crafts, fun. Hang loose . . . invent . . . relax . . . play . . . try something new.

The Fourth-Grader Is a Politician. Having discovered a new life and explored it and even adventured into it, the fourth-grader is ready to try his skills at manipulating people. This is politics. If he manipulates them for the group's benefit, he will become a leader. If he doesn't, he will become unpopular. This is a time when he may find heroes quite different from his parents, yet in some ways very admirable. It is also a time when he very much needs to belong to a small group. If he can be a leader, fine. If he can't, he still wants to belong. Belonging is a big thing. But even when he most intensely wants to be with a gang or a group, he also wants to be alone and have some privacy. He has to talk to himself and listen to himself. Between times he wants to have fun. Show him that mothers and fathers, too, need times to be alone . . . to reflect and gather themselves together. Everyone does!

The Fifth-Grader Is a Producer. Once you find your place among your peers, either as a leader or as a specialized kind of follower with certain skills and abilities, you settle down to produce something. The ability to make something brings a high reward. Children sense which are the central tools of life and which are peripheral. To make this distinction, they rely on their heroes and their parents. Where else can they go for models and for values? In order to clarify their sense of values, they sometimes take to collecting and classifying and naming things. Here is the beginning of systematic knowledge about the world. But in addition to collecting and classifying things, there comes an urge to experiment—to find out what works and what doesn't, what brings pleasure and what brings pain. Can you share with your children your own efforts at production and performance? You yourself need to experiment.

The Sixth-Grader Is a Prince or a Princess. Although the rates of maturation dates may vary between boys and girls and between different cultures and climates, I hold that in the sixth grade we must as parents stand back and see what is happening within our sixth-grader. Whether they have actually arrived or not, this is an age in which all the potentials of independence and sexuality are beginning to emerge. The reason I call them prince or princess is that very soon they will claim the kingdoms of independence and sexuality. Very soon they will be able to create children. Very soon they will be able to get out and earn their own living. This is the great opportunity to help them get ready to carry out these two great tasks of our society with honor and dignity. Now is the time for parents to give their sixth-grader a sense that he or she has a unique value and destiny. Now is the time for both the father and mother to give their sixth-grade boy or girl a sense that it is a splendid thing to be *male* or *female*. Here is also a time when parents can give their child a feeling for the honor and dignity of work—useful work which benefits themselves and others. The sixth-grade boy or girl needs to have a lot of affection from both parents, but even more they need to see Mother and Father affectionate toward each other and proud of each other's role in the family. This helps mightily when the turbulent period of adolescence sets in.

Will you agree that somehow the elementary years of the family are very different from the pre-school years? In a way the pre-school years make the Everyday wonderful. The elementary years make the Wonderful everyday. If you will generously go along with this contrast, then what shall we say about the high school years—seventh grade through twelfth grade? My own view is that in thinking about these next six years, a completely different frame of reference is required which we'll tackle in the next chapter.

12

Your Family Comes of Age

•

THIS MAY STRIKE YOU AS A PECULIAR TITLE because you parents will say, "We've been grown-up for some time! Don't you mean the children?" No, I mean the whole family. During the time the children are moving from their first wet dreams if they're boys, or day of menstruation if they're girls—I mean the time from these dramatic evidences of growing up to the day they leave home for work, or war, or college, or marriage—your family comes of age.

I want to pause a minute right here and make a damaging criticism of our culture. These momentous physical happenings are given the connotation of dirty, smelly, shameful—to be kept secret, hidden, glossed over. Primitive societies are much more in tune with the Creator! They celebrate them. The father may raise a flag over the family hut. God made a miracle. How can we give our adolescent boys and girls a sense of pride and power and joy at these great moments—together with a sense of religious awe? By our own attitudes, of course.

"Adolescence" comes from a Latin word, *alescere*, "to grow." They put an *ad* in front of it to indicate the idea of growing *toward* something or growing *faster* toward a goal. The past participle of the Latin verb *adolescere* is *adultus*, meaning "grown-up." That's the goal. But the words are misleading because no one manages to become perfectly adult, that is, perfectly mature, wise, good, honest, loving, and just. That's what makes it so hard for us to be "good" parents to our adolescent children. From seventh grade through twelfth grade they are driving toward an ideal which we ourselves haven't attained. That's one reason for their impatience with us and for our own embarrassment at their expectations. We may not be so "good" but we are parents and we simply plunge along with them into adolescence and do our best.

Our adolescents have a way of stirring memories and reminding us of certain dreams we held at their age that never came true. Their unreasonable expectations of us bring to the surface of our own consciousness the unreasonable and sometimes cruel ways in which we as adolescents behaved toward our own parents. We thought we had lived these things down, but our own children have the witchcraft to bring these forgotten moments alive within us. They disturb us. This in turn disturbs our children. It echoes through the whole sibling network.

ADOLESCENCE IS A REVOLUTIONARY TIME

It was the best of times, it was the worst of times
It was the age of wisdom, it was the age of foolishness
It was the spring of hope, it was the winter of despair. . . .

This is how Charles Dickens described the French Revolution.

If we were able through some super-electron microscope to observe the infinitely complex chemical, physical, glandular, and structural changes going on within the adolescent's body, we would probably be more patient and understanding. Then, in addition, if we were able on some psychic radar screen to see the resultant feeling changes, the emotional weather patterns, the enormously increased sensitivity, not only to sex stimuli but to all stimuli, we would be even more patient and understanding.

Imagine that you have been flying in a jet for an hour over the great plains—smooth prairies—green pastures—gently rolling farmlands; then suddenly you are over the Grand Canyon. Colors—depths—violent contrasts. A sense of glory and majesty grips you. A fear grips you too—there's no place to land! If you don't keep going, you're lost. That's a little like entering adolescence. Before adolescence, a summer storm simply meant "go home and play in the basement till it's over." But now it may mean:

> O Wild West Wind, thou breath of Autumn's being
> Thou from whose unseen presence the leaves dead
> Are driven like ghosts from an enchanter fleeing,
> Yellow, and black, and pale, and hectic red,
> Pestilence-stricken multitudes!

(Shelley was in an adolescent mood when he wrote these lines celebrating the French Revolution.) That's a new kind of storm. It's a magnified echo of the storm inside you. Before adolescence, dance music goes in one ear and out the other. In fact, it's a bother. Now it goes into you and boils around and makes you want to dance and it rocks you and it rolls you because it corresponds to the emotional turmoil you feel inside yourself and it suggests you can somehow commune with others who are in the same state of storm and stress. It's not a bad idea for parents to let it boil around in them too. The experience can stir up some pretty exciting memories.

THREE KINDS OF GROWING IN ADOLESCENCE

Feelings are enormously important at this age. Adolescents are supersensitive: especially about themselves, their worth, their likability, their interestingness to others, their appearance, the impressions they make, the way they carry themselves. Three questions that teen-agers ask themselves can be used by parents seeking ways and means of helping and strengthening their children moving through adolescence. (By the way, these are serious questions for grown-ups too, including parents.)

How do I really feel about myself? How do I look in the mirror? Picasso's "Girl Before Mirror" is a wonderful statement of this question. Try to think back how you felt about yourself in junior or senior high. I recall going to the shoemaker and having him take off the rubber heels on my new shoes and replace them with leather heels which had steel wedges, so that when I walked down the halls of the school I would create a masculine sound of "click, click, click." At night I studied my nose. It was too wide! I had a protruding front tooth. I imagined that when I came to kissing a girl I might cut her lip. (I had the idea that a kiss must be powerfully implanted or it would be ridiculous.)

Parents, do you remember your very first date? Do you remember how you felt about your own worth? Your own style? I remember when I brought my very first date home, I wondered if I ought to seize her, bend her backward and kiss her "Clark Gable fashion." As we walked toward the door of her home I became almost panicky. I wanted to do what she expected, but I didn't have the vaguest notion of what that might be. At the door I simply shook hands with her and said, "Thanks, Thelma." Feeling inadequate is not limited to adolescents. A Nobel Prize winner told his psychiatrist, "I don't feel I amount to anything." Parents need to help their teen-agers feel they count, are somebody, will amount to something.

How do I really get along with others? From the time your children first began to play with other kids, they have been asking themselves this question. But in adolescence it takes on a new intensity because now it is asked inside a new climate of competition. Now there are at stake two new goals that were not there in the elementary years: 1) Making my way in the world as a person and 2) Finding the mate I want for my life. These goals may not be clearly present in junior high but they begin to emerge in senior high. Even if the plan is to go on to school or work or war, these two goals are hidden realities behind most relationships that are formed at this age.

Relationships are fostered by the ability to identify with another person: that is, the ability to be as interested in the other person as you are in yourself. This is not easy when you still have many confusions and doubts about yourself and have the feeling that you're in revolution, in transition, and in a state of change. Perhaps you should examine the way in which you two parents have related to each other, as your children, while young, were growing and observing you. The relationship between mother and father are among the most significant of all models for children's relationships when their turn comes.

How do I use my freedom? Included in this big question are many smaller ones, like: How do I know what's right and wrong? What are the rules? What are the exceptions? What's worth most? What rights do I have? What rights do others have? How do I reconcile the difference? Do I have some kind of destiny?

Those families who believe in God the Creator of all persons and all things also believe that the Creator gave to all persons: 1) a conscience and 2) free will. If you are a family that lives inside one of the great Judeo-Christian traditions, this may be a good time to examine the "institutionalization of hypocrisy." Adolescents today are peculiarly sensitive to the discrepancies between preaching and practice. For centuries it has been possible to preach and teach that God loves everyone, that he is a God of Justice, that each man is his brother's keeper—and yet to allow millions of nonwhite persons, and millions of povertied persons, to live in a subhuman condition. This came about because hypocrisy was institutionalized, that is, built into cultural and religious institutions. There was the ideal, and there were the understood exceptions. Both the ideal and the exceptions were passed on from generation to generation.

Today something is happening that is terrifying to adults (grown-up, mature persons). It is this: The immature, growing-up persons (adolescents) are saying, "You are hypocrites! You're like the emperor that had no clothes!" Our daughter in the ninth grade came home from a confirmation class on the doctrines of the church very much upset, in fact very mad. I asked her, "Well, what do *you* think you should be studying in your confirmation class?" She looked me in the eye and said with a kind of desperate conviction: "War, race, and poverty." I have to say that at that moment I thought I heard a "word from the Lord" coming to me with blinding clarity from my "immature adolescent" daughter.

Let me ask you: Out of what shall our adolescents build their value systems? In America we adults live in a plethora of "thingful emptiness." Our children don't like it. The Beatles make a song, "The Fool on the Hill." Our children like that. While we adults are busy multiplying our mutual funds, our children are searching for the inner meanings of life. Viktor Frankl, the Viennese psychiatrist, has said, "Life without meaning can lead to insanity." Well, meaning is a human thing. Meaning in life has to do with the way we use our freedom to choose among alternatives so that our actions may benefit ourselves and others simultaneously. *Moral:* Let us parents reexamine our own values before we criticize the values of our own teen-agers.

FIVE DEVILS THAT BUG THE ADOLESCENT

I wince as I read that subtitle. I hear you saying, "Why can't he be constructive and positive? Tell us something good we're doing." You've been reading Spock! Well, I happen to believe most parents know the good things they're doing or trying to do. The trick is to find when good is bad. The road to hell is paved with good intentions. I once heard Paul Tillich say in effect, "The mysterious nature of evil is this: persons of good will with good intentions create structures of evil." A simple example: A family wishing to "do good" becomes so involved in religious, civic, and political crusades that their family life disintegrates. There is no time for it. Or, family income goes up and parents purchase all manner of good things for their children and for themselves. Credit is overextended. The mother goes to a short-term loan shark. As the interest compounds itself, so does her anxiety. Marital tension mounts: Family Service . . . Family Therapy . . . Family Court.

Anyway, here are my five devils:

The Devil of Mistrust. Teen-agers are very keen on detecting inconsistencies in their parents. Not only do they spot contradictions betwen theory and practice, but perhaps more important, between mother and father. Then these contradictions get mingled with their uncertainties about maleness and femaleness. What's valid? What's fake? If parents can somehow find common ground on a few major issues, the teen-ager will be steadied.

Mistrust can also arise from parents' indifference or lack of discipline. Laxness in discipline can be interpreted by teen-age boy or girl as not caring. Failure to praise when praise is due or failure to disapprove when disapproval is appropriate conveys a sense of indifference. Closely related to this is lack of affection and mutual respect between the parents themselves. Do Mom and Dad really care about each other? Do they really respect each other? Teen-agers catch it on their radar screens and draw their own inferences about how marriage is. Sure, you're human, but you can both keep sending out messages that you trust each other and your teen-agers.

The Devil of Shame. "Shame" is a word worth thinking about. It is a painful emotion caused by awareness of some shortcoming or some misbehavior. It is associated with dishonor and disgrace. It has to do with a strong sense of regret. Shame is both good and bad. It is good to feel ashamed if you steal something from a store. Shame is the preface to confession. But what if you can't confess it to anyone? What if you are never forgiven or absolved on the one hand and are never caught and punished on the other? Then shame gets to be a kind of psychic infection. Shame can also arise from misunderstanding and fantasy.

I'll never forget a dreadful summer when I believed I had contracted syphilis from masturbating. I read page after page on syphilis in the Eleventh Edition of the *Encyclopaedia Britannica* and concluded that this was a just punishment for my sin. I considered throwing myself in front of a train. I abandoned the idea because I couldn't figure a way to make it appear accidental. Somehow I got to an understanding medical doctor who in ten minutes miraculously "absolved me of my sin." Now I was free to live again. I was in ninth grade.

The Devil of Guilt. Kenneth Kennison of Yale University has proposed that young people today do not feel so much guilt about sex as they do about violence. He believes that the "bomb," the wars, the revolutions occurring every month somewhere in the world, the riots in America, the shows of force by student groups, are very disturbing to adolescents. The reason is that the adolescent is in a revolutionary state himself. He has fantasies of destruction. He dreams of clearing away authorities, establishments, and structures because they seem incapable of carrying out obviously needed changes. But this involves attacking many persons that the adolescent loves, respects, and depends on. So his guilt rises. So the generation gap widens. So parents become defensive and try to prove you can't do anything really good outside the authority structures of the many establishments.

It is well for parents of adolescents to do a bit of thinking on the amount of sheer violence in history and in today's world. The American land was cleared of the Indian by violence. The whole criminal world operates by the rules of violence. The whole police system operates as a movement of counterviolence. What shall be our response to violence? What if Justice is blind and deaf? How shall seeing and hearing be restored? Let us parents reflect whether we feel guilt about the right wrongs.

The Devil of Inferiority. In a strenuously competitive system, how can everyone possibly be a winner? The law of the normal curve says that there will be as many below average as above average. Beginning in first grade, we humiliate the slow learners. They are "Ducks." The average are "Blue Jays." The top group are "Cardinals." Social stratification sets in. Inferiority is felt.

William James spoke of the American "bitch-goddess of Success." What is it really that is so bitchy about success? It is the idea that your success involves someone else's failure. It is the idea of the law of the jungle in an age when the United Nations is trying to help nations rise above cutthroat competition.

Why do teen-age boys especially drop out of school? They are made to feel so inferior they can't stand it. The American man is supposed to be able to "go out and sell the product." What if you're shy? What if you're below average in guts? What if you believe the product is a fake?

There is indeed in our schools a movement to recognize the unique value and worth of each individual teen-ager. Parents need to reinforce this movement. They need to discover the peculiar interests and the particular dreams hidden away in their own teen-agers. They need to respect and resonate to these interests and dreams. They need to refrain from drawing unfavorable comparisons. They need to cooperate with the Creator in bringing forth whatever is "tightly folded up" within each young man and woman. They are to help them unfold their ultimate possibilities for good.

TOWARD THE NEW LIFE

Erich Fromm gave a great lecture at Roosevelt College in Chicago years ago. I have to rely on my memory. It was never published. He began by describing the inhuman practices of idol worship:

1) Baal-worship, which consisted of mass sex orgies in which everyone violated as many others as he was able to.

2) Mammon-worship, which consisted in a kind of King Midas fixation on money for its own sake.

3) Moloch-worship, which consisted of burning your own children to secure superhuman powers.

Suddenly he stopped short and asked, "Do you think Americans

worship these same idols and practice these hideous sacrifices?"
The audience was quiet. Then he said, in effect:

1) Our fantastic exaggeration of physical sex is Baal-worship.

2) Our eternal search for more money and property is Mammon-worship.

3) Our perpetual quest for power over people is Moloch-worship.

He ended with a heartrending analogy. Primitive idol worship
tore marriages apart, destroyed the lives of children, and ruined
family life. Modern idol worship is doing the same. Is it possible
that we parents are involved in idol worship that separates us
from each other and from our children?

But Erich Fromm is no mere prophet of doom. He is also a
bringer of good news. In his little classic, *The Art of Loving,* he
examines the many modern misunderstandings of love. Having
done so, he goes on to say that when you really love someone, you
become profoundly concerned about helping that person unfold
and develop and become the full human being that the Creator
in a mysterious manner hoped for. And this helping process, says
Fromm, will also give you a profound sense of fulfillment.

I find that I can use this germinal idea in thinking about my
own way of loving my wife. But my wife and I can also use it in
thinking about the way in which we love our own and all adolescents.

13

Your Family Begins a New Life

•

Now BEGINS THE WHOLE PROCESS of sending your children off—to work or to war or to marriage or to college. It isn't so much that you must send them as that they know very well they *must go.* They know it. You know it. It's something like when you, Mother, gave birth to them. The time came when they were to be born. You pushed them out with profound labor. But you knew it had to be if they were to live. Now you both know they have to leave home if they are going to become full adults, make it on their own, chart and sail their own course on the sea of life.

There are a couple of ideas about this launching time that may be worth thinking about. For instance, something called the "psychosocial moratorium." Really, this begins in senior high and may run through the college years or the equivalent years in the military service or at work or even in marriage. The idea is that young people toward the end of their adolescence need more elbow room than they do before or after. They need to experiment and try themselves out without being severely censured. A friend of mine is an eminent rural sociologist. We were discussing the meaning of boys stealing cars. He reflected that, as a boy in Montana, he and a group of ranchers' sons would "borrow" horses and ride them until they were just about done for. But it wasn't classed as "horse stealing." The old ranchers would say "The boys have to have some way to blow off steam." How can you help your older children blow off steam and yet not be hauled into court and sent to jail? You can't safely treat them as children when they're nearly adult!

Another idea worth thinking about is something called "separation anxiety." It simply means the mixture of intense hope and intense fear that beset the young boy or girl as they know they must set out on their own. Will they make it or won't they? Closely linked to this feeling is the feeling of ambivalence. Ambivalence means feeling two ways at once, for instance feeling that your parents are very dear and feeling that they are disgusting. They are great people: they are numbskulls. They are wonderful: they are cabbage-heads. What do these contradictory feelings (and the actions that go with them) mean? Well, they wish they could stay dependent and protected and safe. But they also hope they will be able to "kiss them off and bug out . . . forget 'em and start fresh." There is a powerful drive forward to be themselves. There is also a powerful pull backward to the "rock from which you were hewn and the quarry from which you were cut." This makes for ambivalence and separation anxiety.

THE SCATTERING OF THE FLOCK

It is not a big bad wolf that scatters your flock of children; it is the whirlwind of modern American society. Recently I met a mother of four daughters, all married. The family was of English ancestry and had come up through the Episcopal way of believing. She described with affection her four sons-in-law: 1) Russian-Jewish, 2) Norwegian-Lutheran, 3) Swedish-Methodist, 4) Polish-Catholic. This tells me something about a theology of creation— the meeting of persons rather than of structures. There was in these boys and girls something of the "Image of God" that was powerfully attractive in spite of their extremely different backgrounds. I ask you *what was it* that attracted them? I believe it was their complementarity, the "goodness" that they found in each other.

This same mother reported that she had just finished her semi-annual visit with each of her daughters. They live in 1) California, 2) Texas, 3) Missouri, 4) Maine. She proudly showed pictures of her many grandchildren. "I talk with them by phone about once a month," she said. I know another grandmother who keeps in touch with her scattered flock by extensive letter writing. Some families stage annual reunions; others every three years or so. Even in severely disorganized families there is a tremendous need to come home for the holidays. If the mutual concern and love within the family has been strong, ways will be found to maintain meaningful relationships no matter how scattered the flock may be.

THE MIXING OF FAITHS AND CULTURES, CLASSES AND RACES

A friend of mine was raised in the Ukrainian Orthodox Church. His mother is a famous "writer" of Ukrainian Easter eggs. He married a Norwegian Lutheran girl. Now his mother dearly wishes her grandchildren to treasure these wonderful Easter eggs. So the young bride does her best to learn the intricate, time-consuming ritual. Her heart isn't in it. The young husband is a true and faithful father. He defends the right of his wife to cook up her own Easter rituals. They must begin together. They must work out their own new ways to celebrate "New Life."

At graduation time a high school classmate of mine phoned and said he'd like to visit us. We said, "Come on out." "We're here for the graduation of our son-in-law," he said. "Well of course, all of you come out," I said. The son-in-law was a black, professionally trained, social worker married to a very blond Norwegian Lutheran. We found out that the black parents had objected to the marriage. However, they were persuaded to visit the white farm family for a weekend. When they got to know the white family of the prospective bride, they felt differently about the whole thing. The fluidity of American society does not only mix cultures and faiths and races. It also mixes classes: the rich and the poor. Some speak of a "meritocracy"—a society where persons rise to leadership because of innate ability, capacity, and generosity. This becomes more and more of a possible reality as society helps those with innate ability to go to school and to develop their talents and to express them openly.

FATHER AND MOTHER BECOME "GRAND-"

In all languages the words for grandfather and grandmother carry some special quality of esteem. When you become part of this "grand" class, you are free from petty jealousy. You no longer worry if the grandchild looks more like "your side" or the "other side." You simply love and let go. You have arrived at the stage of maturity where you can say with Harry Golden, "Enjoy! Enjoy!" But "grand"-parents do more than tickle their grandchildren to make them laugh or give them the candy that their parents disapprove of; they can sit and observe them with a kind of awe impossible for their own parents. They can view them from the faraway perspective of the Creator Himself. They are filled with a sense of reverence and delight and awe and joy.

The beneficent grandparents are those who leave parenting to the parents while they observe the good points of their grandchildren. Grandparents pray for their children and for their grandchildren because they have the vision to see their own hopes and dreams carried forward into the third generation. If they are asked for advice and counsel, they give it. If not, they simply observe and make mental notes of the ongoing works of the Creator.

FATHER AND MOTHER BECOME "WISDOM GIVERS"

When you become grandparents (unless your children and grandchildren live very near you), you can't spend all your time with them. You can now have a new life and a free life! You have a lifetime of learning behind you. What will you do with it? Will you hide it under an umbrella of modesty or will you give it to some young couple who have moved so far and so many times that they are utterly alone in their new world? Are you able to adopt them as your "foster children"?

Let me propose the idea: All around you there are newlyweds. They have met in some place far from the bride's home, far from the husband's home. They fall in love, and marry. They move and begin to create a home. They need friends, young or old. They need ideas to make their new home interesting. They need somebody to talk to besides each other. Find these young couples. Invite them over simply because you believe in marriage and family life. Find out what they are hoping for. Help them realize their hopes. Stand by them. Sponsor them. If they seem willing, adopt them, especially when they have no nearby parents to support their hopes and dreams. If you get too close, they'll let you know.

Young parents need the friendship of couples similar in age to their own parents, who may be a thousand miles away. It's not so much to find out exactly *how* to treat the sick baby (the pediatrician will do that) or even exactly how to discipline the three-year-old who won't mind (experience will do that). It's more to give a sense of the continuity of life—from one generation to the other. We are in a time of tremendously rapid change. That's what makes it so important that you find young families and become "wisdom givers" to them in the best sense. You will bless each other more than you can believe.

The two of you may be in touch with newlyweds and young families, but you can't spend all your time on them. What can you do with your free time? I believe the calendar is very important for grandparents. A calendar that tells when everyone's birthday and anniversary is coming up. A thoughtful message will mean more than a splendid present. You may now engage in causes or enter into hobbies or indulge yourselves in interests that you never felt fully free "to let yourself go into" before. You have one life to live. "Enjoy! Enjoy!" God made the world for fun.

A fantastic change has come about in American family life in the last half century. Fifty years ago one parent was dead when the last child left home. Today the average married couple will have as many years together alone as they had raising their children. What shall they do with this new-found time of life?

Obviously it's up to them—*you*, that is. If you have lots of stocks and bonds, you can clip coupons. If you believe in clean air and clean water for the coming generations, you can work on conservation and pollution control. If you believe in metropolitan government, you can work on that. If you believe in helping the poor, there are plenty of them to help. If you like art or music, bring some kids along and introduce them to a new world. Or just go alone and enjoy the day. If you like politics, now is the time to read up on the issues, to help your candidate and to support good, new laws and movement for reform.

Make common cause with other persons who are in your own stage of life. Don't sit home and watch the "boob tube" all the time. Go calling. Invite people over for coffee. Plant flowers, watch them grow, exchange cuttings, show off your goldfish, entertain children in the block, thank God you are alive and still able to sense and enjoy this multifarious creation and all his creatures.

WE PREPARE FOR THE "LONG SLEEP"

Death can intrude itself into any family at any stage of life. A child may be stillborn. There may be a miscarriage. A teen-ager may be killed on his motorcycle. A college co-ed may be killed in a car accident. A son may be killed in military action. A young mother may die of leukemia. A young father may be killed in a hunting accident. Death is present everywhere.

But if you have escaped death and lived to become grandparents and are looking toward the inevitable end, there are many interesting things you can do. Whether you are together as a married couple or whether you are alone because your mate is gone, you can do two enormously important things:

1) You can love and worship God—alone or with others in your own way.

2) You can love and serve your neighbor—one to one or with others who wish to.

You can live in the belief that you were created *for others* and you can seek out someone who is alone, without loved ones. You shall love your neighbor as yourself! I believe the Creator has implanted this into every human being. Everyone responds to it.

You can reflect on the mysterious fact that all persons are made out of this earth on which we were born, on which we live, on which we find our purpose in life. It follows as the night the day that we are destined to return to this earth.

But above all these considerations there towers the supreme fact of faith: he who created us and has watched over us throughout our whole life will take charge of us when we enter the "Long Sleep." If he created us, he will receive us at the "End of Days." He will transform us into something meaningful in his vast purpose and design.

PART IV

•

BUILDING YOUR FAMILY
INTO THE COMMUNITY

14

Your Neighborhood and School

•

JEROME D. AND BESSIE S. FOLKMAN

Jerome and Bessie Folkman, married thirty-nine years, have three children and eight grandchildren. Jerome is Rabbi of Temple Israel, Columbus, Ohio, teaches in the Sociology Department of Ohio State University, is the author of numerous articles and the books *Design for Jewish Living* and *Marriage Has Many Faces*. He has been involved in many local and national projects; among them he was Chairman of the Committee on Marriage, Home, and Family for the Central Conference of American Rabbis, 1950–58; President of the Ohio Conference on Family Relations, 1955–57; member of the Executive Committee of the National Council on Family Relations, 1961–63. Bessie Schomer Folkman has been for years consistently active in local and national social works and foundations, e.g., National Foundation for Infantile Paralysis, Board Member of Multiple Sclerosis Society and of the Children's Psychiatric Center. She has been the recipient of several awards for such services, including the Merit Mother of Ohio Award in 1966, and the Community Service Award of the Urban League Guild, 1968. She was co-author of *Democracy and Religion Begin at Home*, which is now in its second, revised, edition.

•

MANY DEFINITIONS OF "COMMUNITY" ARE OFFERED by social scientists. But, for religious purposes, the definitions of the social scientists are not always adequate. Universal religions like Judaism and Christianity conceive of the whole world as a single community with God as the universal Father and all humanity as His children. Science is limited by reality while religion is fundamentally concerned with the ideal.

The dichotomy between the real and the ideal was bridged by Hillel, a first-century rabbinical teacher. He said: "If I am not for myself, who will be for me? Yet if I am for myself only, what am I? And if not now, when?" The sage recognized that maturation in a person requires both self-reliance and the ability to relate one's self to others. The whole person must know himself, his abilities, and his limitations; at the same time, he cannot be a total personality if his self-interests constitute the horizons of his world.

This dual process begins in the home. The family is the first social group with which the child identifies himself. The family offers the child his first social experience. Within the scope of family life, the child grows and is imprinted with the values, ideals, aspirations, methods, language, and communication symbols shared by other members of the family with the growing child and with each other. If the family is founded upon love, the love of the husband and the wife for each other and their love as parents for their children, the probability is high that the youthful members of the family will learn to love each other and later love their fellowmen. Those who are compelled to grow up without a loving parental example are deprived and disadvantaged indeed. Without such an imprint upon their personalities, young people grow up handicapped with respect to their ability to relate themselves to others. The home is a microcosm; the probabilities are great that the attitudes and values imprinted at home will characterize the manner in which each individual member of the family relates himself or herself to the neighborhood of which the family is a part and, indeed, to the world itself, which has become an enlarged neighborhood or composite of neighborhoods.

But love is not enough. No community can operate without

law, without regulations that will protect individuals from others as well as themselves, defend communities from the antisocial acts of individuals, and individuals from organized communities. There can be no social organization without regulation or law; this applies with equal force to the family. Early in the twentieth century, American families could and did operate on an authoritarian basis; the typical American family was as patriarchal as Hebrew families in Bible times. The father proclaimed the rules and regulations within which the family would function and made all important decisions when unexpected problems emerged. Within two decades, the twentieth-century American family needed a different kind of structure. The typical American father is an absentee. If he is asked to make rules or decisions, he may be inclined to follow the example of his own father who lived in a world entirely different from that in which the contemporary family must survive.

Very few modern families can operate within an authoritarian structure. In the model American family today, rules and regulations are established by the father and mother with full consideration of the personalities and needs of each of the children and frequently in consultation with them. The regulations are not spontaneous or capricious; they are the result of experience and the anticipation of future problems. The family policies must be explicitly formulated; implicit rules might not be recognized by every member of the family. Each member of the family, especially younger ones, must be made aware of things done in their family and those things not done. Personality disturbances frequently occur in families in which there is no explicit regulation and in families in which there is excessive regulation, or in which the regulation is spontaneous, capricious, or unstable.

In a general atmosphere of love and affection, within a framework of regulation, the individual must have sufficient freedom of choice and initiative to prepare him for subsequent participation and involvement in the larger community of which the family is only a part. Overcontrolled individuals do not readily learn to adapt themselves to the free, democratic society. Sometimes, they become authoritarian personalities requiring a constant domination and control from another, or domination and control over others. Sometimes they become resentful of all social organization; they are readily recognized as chronic "aginners." A similar resentfulness of social organization may be manifested by those whose domestic environment was lawless, unregulated, and anarchical.

Personalities nurtured in loving and affectional families with no more and no less regulation than necessary, with abundant opportunity for individual initiative and innovation, are generally better able to identify themselves with groups outside the family but upon which families depend for intellectual, spiritual, and social support and protection. Personalities maturing in families deficient in love, regulation, and opportunities for the expression of the individual initiative will be "undernourished," suffering from deficits that cannot easily be made up through affiliation with other groups outside the family.

Churches and synagogues, like other voluntary community organizations, seem to attract many such persons who are trying to discover there what was denied them in their early family experience. Such efforts are rarely successful and often subvert social and religious organizations ostensibly dedicated to the noblest purposes. The best adjustments and the most fruitful contributions to social organizations are made by those whose basic personality structures developed in loving, affectional, well-regulated families in which individuality was held sacred.

COMMUNITY CLUBS

The development of community clubs or block organizations has been an interesting phenomenon in the American urban community. In the earlier rural communities, primary relationships were the rule. Most people knew each other on an eye-to-eye, first-name basis. Urban organizations, like Rotary and Kiwanis Clubs, have tried to revive the primary relationship by requiring the use of first names at meetings. These contrived efforts are not always successful; the fallacy is exposed when the wives of members are invited to club parties or other social activities. The wives seem to be more sensitive to differentiations in social class positions or status. Many of the community service clubs have established ladies' auxiliaries among the wives of their members in order to bridge these gaps.

Community clubs and block organizations have the advantage of drawing their membership from a specified, geographically limited locale. Common concerns are generally coincidental functions of the common situations. Deteriorating neighborhoods offer lower housing costs and rentals, attracting the less affluent. Unwilling to stand idly by while their investments in their homes diminish through depreciation, or desiring for their families more favorable living conditions, or both, residents in these neighborhoods may form block organizations to achieve these aims and frequently discover others. In more affluent, middle-class communities, clubs are formed, generally for recreational purposes. A community swimming pool may be undertaken; adequate supervision and maintenance are essential and appropriate assessments are made upon the members for the proper maintenance of the facilities they establish. In some of these communities, the "private" nature of the organizations facilitates restrictions against the "undesirables" who may be members of minority ethnic or racial groups. Other community clubs have been organized by socially conscious community leaders. These leaders give character to their communities. It is not unusual to find two adjacent but very different suburban communities in the same metropolitan area. Even though each consists of individuals and families at approximately the same social, educational, and cultural levels, one might be expulsivistic and bigoted while the other might pride itself on its open membership and universal idealism.

SCHOOL

Jerome is fond of repeating the story of the manner in which his own mother introduced him to public school experience. Other than his indoctrination at home, he had no pre-school experience. His earliest recollections of childhood included memories of discussions about the privilege of going to school. Again and again he heard that in many European countries Jews were denied the right to go to school, or were very much restricted in opportunities available to them. He heard that in America the right to education was free and open to all. The first day of school was almost a holy day for him. On that day, his mother escorted her five-year-old son to the elementary school in which his kindergarten class would meet. On the way to school, she pointed out landmarks by which he could guide himself when it became his task to go to school by himself. The second day, his mother suggested that he go first— alone. She assured him that she would be following close behind, but she would not interrupt him or help him unless he was doing something very wrong or dangerous. His success in finding his own way to school on the second day was crowned by his mother's felicitations at the end of the trip. On the third day of school, this five-year-old boy went to kindergarten and returned home by himself, feeling twenty-five years of age!

Certainly, that mother loved her son, but her love was not the clinging, demanding, holding, restraining kind. She made the rules for going to school explicit. She explained the way to school in terms of landmarks a preliterate could understand. Then she tested her son's ability to find his own way before she sent him to kindergarten by himself. No one who knew her would say that she was not worried on the third day that her son went to school by himself, without any adult direction or assistance. But she did not want her son tied to her apron strings! She did not want to rear an utterly dependent personality.

In kindergarten class, the boy discovered a friend who lived nearby. Soon, the two boys were going to school and coming home together. This arrangement met with the approval of the mothers of both boys. One day, with rain threatening, the kindergartner donned his new raincoat before he left for school. It was made of sturdy material, and his five-year-old fingers had difficulty working the buttons into their holes.

Once at school, he was able to unbutton the raincoat with ease. When the session of the kindergarten class was over, the sun had come out and the rainclouds had completely vanished. Nevertheless, the kindergarten teacher insisted that every raincoat be buttoned so that the class might give a neat and orderly appearance as they marched out of the building behind the national colors to the music of the piano played in the main hall by the principal herself. This little boy could not button his raincoat without help. The teacher insisted he should. He was reluctant to try because he was afraid of the embarrassment of failure in the presence of his classmates who seemed to have none of these difficulties. The teacher waited as long as she could, and then she said, "We can't wait any longer for you, Jerome; the class will have to march out, while you learn to button your raincoat." The boy's weeping was amplified; it became screaming and yelling but to no avail. The teacher returned to her classroom and seated herself at her desk to do her paper work. The kindergartner voiced his objections to her policy as loudly as he could.

The kindergartner's friend was loyal; he was not afraid of guilt by association with a crybaby. He went back into the school building and tried to help his friend button the raincoat to fulfill the requirements of the teacher for his release from the kindergarten classroom. In the meantime, the boys' mothers were alarmed at their failure to return home at the usual time. They decided to walk to school to discover whether their sons were loitering on the way. The mother of the crying kindergartner later told how relieved she was when she heard the screams of her son. "That's my Jerome," she said; "he must be all right."

The mothers went into the building. As soon as the boy saw his mother, his screams were augmented. Calmly the teacher explained that it was essential for a big boy in school to learn to button his own raincoat. She also conceded that it was most kind and considerate of his friend to help him. The mothers left the building. The crying stopped, and the boy buttoned his coat! These mothers did not interfere with the socialization of their sons under the direction of the public school teacher. They did not circulate petitions or offer resolutions for her dismissal. They respected her authority, and one of the most important lessons of that kindergarten class was well taught and thoroughly learned.

Teacher is not always right, of course. No one is. But the teacher is entitled to the respect of parents which will be reflected in respectful attitudes of students. Parents who act on the assumption that the teacher is wrong deny her an opportunity to accomplish what she is trying to achieve. When a mistake is made by a teacher or by a member of the educational apparatus, more harm than good will be done by the parents who vent their wrath in the presence of their offspring. Teachers and principals can be consulted without the knowledge of the children and certainly not in their presence. Parents should not be hesitant about making inquiries regarding the instruction of their children; they need not deny themselves the right of voicing objections as long as they find themselves in strong disagreement. But their children ought not be witnesses to such dissension.

Parents should not be inhibited in the desire to help their children with their schoolwork. The ideal teaching situation is "the teacher at one end of the log with the pupil at the other." In our mass society with its adverse teacher-pupil ratios, opportunities for such situations are rare. Parents can be helpful if they know how. With the parent as a teacher's aide, the ideal teaching situation can be approximated. If school administrations or parent-teacher organizations could offer parents instruction in the ways of helpfulness to their children, the levels of educational effectiveness could be raised immeasurably. When new methods are being used, parents ought to be indoctrinated by effectual introductions to them; then parents would not be cast in opposition roles. Many children capable of mathematical procedures at the third or fourth grade levels look contemptuously upon parents who graduated from high school and perhaps even from college without being able to understand the symbolic language of the "new math." Such role reversals have morbid effects on both the schools and the lives of the families whose children constitute the student bodies.

When the school health authorities discover health problems, especially in seeing or hearing, these should be called to the attention of both parents and teachers without delay. Children who seem intelligent enough in other ways but who experience learning handicaps when reading or hearing or both are involved ought to have a physical examination before they are labeled "slow learners." Parents who have knowledge of physical handicaps, visual or auditory limitations, ought to be sure that their information is shared with school authorities, subject to validation, of course. Many a child has been handicapped for years and sometimes for a lifetime by the label "slow learner" or "retarded" when a correctable visual or auditory defect is his only barrier to normal or better than average achievement.

The "tongue thrust" appears to be learned behavior which gives the child the appearance of being dull or stupid. The child who is repeatedly treated as if he were dull may actually become what he seems to be. A speech therapist can help the child to unlearn the tongue-thrusting habit. Such therapy is essential to successful orthodontics and important to the child's socialization.

The national war on poverty has discovered that children from culturally deprived, intellectually disadvantaged and economically impoverished homes are frequently handicapped as severely as those who suffer from visual, auditory or other physical defects. Poverty has been defined as a "subculture" in this country; children from such disadvantaged homes find themselves poorly equipped for school experience. They have not had the experience of middle-class children; so the "Dick and Jane" vocabulary requires concepts completely foreign to them. Handicapped before their entrance into school, these children are unhappy there. They feel alien and unwanted. These feelings are frequently exacerbated by teachers who would much rather be assigned to schools in the more affluent neighborhoods. Antisocial behavior is not uncommon among these children. If they can manage to get through school without being involved in too many disciplinary problems, they are fortunate indeed. Suspensions and expulsions are not uncommon among them. Many of them become dropouts. Usually the deficit seems beyond repair by the time they discover how limited the need is in this highly advanced technological society for people without even a secondary education.

Consequently, poverty tends to become self-perpetuating. Education, the principal exit from this "subculture," is denied them or rejected by them. Poverty and its attendant social problems have become the most serious challenge to the survival of the American democracy.

One inner-city clergyman observed that the children in the neighborhood of his church needed help with their schoolwork more than they needed anything else. He engaged a competent teacher and advertised supervised study classes in his church for all the children of the neighborhood regardless of race or creed. Response to this offering astonished everyone, including the pastor. The teacher required assistance. The congregation had been persuaded to indulge the pastor and to permit the expenditure of congregational funds for the engagement of a qualified teacher for the after-school hours, but they were reluctant to appropriate any more funds from a budget which they believed to be committed to exclusively "religious" purposes. The pastor consulted with the College of Education in the state university located in the same city; it was agreed that the teacher engaged was qualified as a supervisor, so education students could be assigned to her for their practical experience. The study hall was a great success.

When the bishop heard about it, he was perturbed. These were secular studies. Were they appropriate for church sponsorship? He decided to make a visitation. He was profoundly impressed by what he saw. It was difficult for him to believe that these children could possibly be so interested in supervised study. He was convinced by his discussions with the children and their teachers. Later, in the pastor's study, he confronted the young minister with this fundamental problem: "All this is good enough," the bishop said, "but how does this activity advance the Church of Christ?"

"Sir," the young minister replied as politely as he possibly could, "if these children were starving and we organized our church facilities to serve them hot lunches, would you ask me whether such an activity advanced the cause of Christ?" The point was conceded by the bishop. "If these children were naked," the minister continued, "and the congregation organized an agency for the distribution of clothing to them, would you question the activity?"

"Certainly not!" the bishop replied.

"Then, sir, I submit that these children are in greater need of education than of food or clothing. Our church is committed to the task of supplying this most urgent need." The bishop put his hand on the pastor's shoulder.

"God bless you, my son," he said.

A public school teacher in another inner-city school told of her experience with her students in the trying times that followed the tragic assassination of the late Martin Luther King, Jr., in 1968. It mattered little to her that her students were all racially different from her. They were children of the living God, and she loved them. She was not pestering her superiors for another assignment; even when one was offered to her, she declined it. She felt that these Negro children needed her more than children in the more fashionable, middle-class neighborhoods. Once the students discovered her sincerity and total commitment, their acceptance of her became one of the school's most widely known traditions.

On the day after the assassination, disorders occurred in many American cities. The students in this particular school decided to strike; the word was passed on their grapevine that no black students would attend class the next day. Instead, they would form picket lines at the school entrances. When her students told her what was going to happen, she asked, "Why strike against the school? After all, the school had nothing to do with the tragedy." The students insisted that the school was part of the social system that made the work of men like Martin Luther King necessary, and consequently, the school shared the guilt of the racist society. The teacher tried in vain to dissuade her students.

"Give us one good reason why we should not strike," one of the students challenged.

"For one thing," the teacher replied, "a strike against the school would be illegal. The law requires the attendance of students unless they are specifically excused." The students laughed.

"Martin Luther King was not afraid to violate laws," said one of them. "He went to jail many times."

"But he finished his education first!" said the teacher, triumphantly scoring her point. The students agreed to attend class the next day in spite of the strike in which most of the other students would participate.

Realistically, the teacher knew that her students would be subjected to the ridicule and scorn of their striking peers. They would be called "scabs" and worse. She decided that there would have to be another and more appropriate expression of sorrow and grief planned for the next day. Discussion with the students revealed their support of her proposal. The major activity in the class the next morning would be a memorial to the fallen Negro leader. She had succeeded in impressing upon her students the importance of education at the same time that she helped them to provide an expression for their very profound feelings of outrage and grief.

Because of the tremendous importance of education in the socialization of children, especially in a society as complex as ours, much is expected of the school. Some seem to expect too much of the school! At best, the school is adjunct to the home. The formal educational apparatus can stand only upon the base provided by the home.

Almost two decades ago, Dr. Harold Alberty, of Ohio State University, and some of his graduate students undertook a study of the attacks upon the American educational system. In their survey, they discovered that the basic criticisms could be summarized under ten general statements:

1) Schools are not effectively teaching children the fundamental skills.
2) Schools are not developing obedience, respect for authority, a sense of responsibility, or a sense of the importance of hard work.
3) Schools fail to stimulate competition among students and to reveal to parents the comparative standing of their children.
4) Schools are trying to educate many young people who cannot profit sufficiently from such education.
5) Schools have not been effective in interpreting their programs to the public.
6) Schools fail to develop a wholehearted allegiance to the American way of life.
7) Schools are taking over the functions and responsibilities of the home and other institutions.
8) Schools are not teaching boys and girls to make a living.
9) Schools are not keeping pace with social change.

10) School personnel are not competent to deal with complex problems the modern school faces.

The internal inconsistencies in these attacks are obvious. Nevertheless, they are still being aired almost two decades later. One more serious charge has been made: "American public schools are so biased in the direction of the white middle class that others are handicapped in the American educational system." In many communities, heroic efforts have been made to repair some of these alleged defects, and some successes have been achieved. Nevertheless, these criticisms point the way to necessary amelioration. Parent-Teacher Associations offer parents, teachers, and school administrators opportunities for such constructive criticism and reform where indicated. Parental interest and concern for the welfare of the schools enhance them in the eyes of children. Parents who participate in these activities ought to let their children know of their interest and concern without prejudicing them against teachers and schools.

Another way in which parents and other concerned citizens can give positive assistance to the community's educational apparatus is through the support of tax levies and bond issues designed to provide adequate finances for public education. In most American communities, members of the teaching profession are compensated at rates lower than those received in other professions and occupations by people with similar or less academic preparation, training, and experience. Members of the teaching professions are often reluctant to organize for collective bargaining; teachers' strikes have occurred, but they rarely receive the public response that their organizers anticipated. Parents and other concerned citizens ought to take upon themselves the responsibility for doing for the teachers of the children of their community what the educators are hardly able to do for themselves. Many competent persons would be attracted to the teaching professions if they could be assured of a decent living. Those who feel called to teach may not place a monetary reward at the top of their value hierarchies, but they do not want their families to be utterly handicapped in their own quest of the good life.

THE VANISHING NEIGHBORHOOD

Increasing difficulties experienced by proponents of school levies and bond issues may be explained in part by the vanishing neighborhood, the diminishing sense of community. In the modern American urban community, it is not uncommon for dwellers in the same high-rise apartment buildings to be without any acquaintance in the same buildings. Owners and residents of homes on city streets not uncommonly spend many years there without ever visiting in one another's homes or coming to know one another personally. This diminished sense of community contributes to the vanishing idea of "neighborhood." To reverse this trend, many neighborhood leaders have developed organizations for neighborhood activities and observances.

In one American community, two neighbors discussed the noisiness and peril in the neighborhood on the Fourth of July; they decided to have a neighborhood celebration on the morning of Independence Day in order that the noise and fireworks might be confined to those hours so that the rest of the day could be enjoyed in relative peace and quiet. They interested other neighbors in the project, organized a parade of residents of all ages, and even formed a band of those in the area who could play movable instruments. The celebration was concluded with community singing, patriotic addresses, and adequately controlled fireworks. The neighbors discovered that they enjoyed each other's company and friendship so much that the plan for the observance of the Fourth of July became a medium for the revival of the sense of community.

It must be noted that the preparations for the neighborhood celebration stimulated many family discussions well in advance of the Fourth of July. The neighborhood observance was effective principally because of the involvement of family units. Such organizations have become extremely popular in many American communities.

Similar neighborhood organizations have been directed toward the development of community pride and concern. Some have involved children and adults in clean-up campaigns and other techniques for community appreciation and improvement. In some cases, parental instructions within a particular family will affect a larger community. Formal organization is not always necessary, but it is an aid to communication and sharing of experience. When the authors had young children in their home, they evolved a unique way of managing the bicycles, wagons, and other small vehicles used by the children in the household. The family held a council for the discussion of the problem. The dangers of leaving vehicles on sidewalks and driveways were spelled out. Various suggestions were made by members of the family; some of the younger members proposed the parking of vehicles in the garage or in the basement. Other members of the family voiced their objections on the grounds of impracticability. The garage was not large enough to accommodate the family's two cars and the bicycles and wagons. Moreover, the perils were still present. Removing bicycles and wagons to the basement was simply out of the question! It was decided that the family ought to have a rule requiring bicycles, wagons, and other small vehicles to be parked on the grass lawn as carefully as possible. Then the question of enforcement was considered. It was decided that tickets should be issued and attached to the vehicles of the offenders. A fine of one cent was prescribed for the first offense, two cents for the second, and three cents for the third. In actuality, the fine for the second offense never had to be imposed. A penny was money in those days!

On one occasion, an offender objected to the ticket on his bicycle and demanded the right to be heard in the matter. He based his objection on the argument that he was being punished for something he did not do. He had loaned his bicycle to his friend Jimmy, and Jimmy parked the bicycle illegally but unknowingly. The father explained that ownership involves responsibility.

"I take an appeal," declared the son. This had never occurred before in the family discussions. The family had never before experienced the questioning of its authority in this way. Fortunately a Superior Court judge lived across the street. He was invited to review the case. With citations of the law and references to decisions of the State Supreme Court, the learned judge upheld the decision. As long as the bicycle had not been stolen or used contrary to the will of the owner, the owner was certainly responsible. Soon the incident was being discussed on the street; what began as a household rule later became a block regulation.

The neighborhood is not an anachronism. It can be revived by people with imagination and initiative. Its rewards are legion. Its costs are minimal.

15

Your "Causes" and Civic Participation

•

ALEXIS DE TOCQUEVILLE, nineteenth-century French statesman and political writer, studied the newly established United States of America and made some remarkable observations; one of these was the way in which the people of the newborn republic solved their problems. Unlike their Old World counterparts, Americans formed committees and organizations instead of petitioning the governmental authorities for remedial programs.

In the predominantly rural society de Tocqueville studied, communities were small and neighborhoods were intimate. Many problems were solved through voluntary cooperation and neighborly helpfulness. When sickness or misfortune afflicted a family, relatives and neighbors would immediately come to their help. No social work investigations were necessary because the helpers and the helped knew each other very well and the roles could easily have been reversed. Children witnessed the neighborliness, helpfulness and cooperation extended by their parents to those in need; the example was profoundly imprinted upon them. When their teachers or their clergy taught and preached to them about charity, kindness, and neighborliness, the words evoked memories stored in their minds. It never occurred to preachers or teachers that it was necessary to teach commitment, involvement, or civic responsibility.

The voluntary personal or organized activities of American citizens covered the major burden of responsibility for philanthropy and social improvements in the United States until the depression of the thirties. Then, welfare needs reached such tremendous proportions that voluntary efforts barely scratched the surface. At first, relief of economic distress was regarded as a purely local responsibility; when voluntary efforts fell short of the needs, local governments became involved. Cities and counties found themselves in bitter controversies regarding their proportionate shares of responsibility for relief. In most cases, the total efforts of both were inadequate and the federal government entered into the welfare and relief work on a national scale under the constitutional "general welfare" clause. Although the subject is still controversial among some segments of the American population, the federal government now carries the lion's share of the responsibilities for health, education, and welfare, and a member of the President's Cabinet is the head of a federal department dedicated to this work.

Even the work of voluntary agencies is carried on outside of the home, so that members of the family rarely observe the work they are asked to support by their private, voluntary contributions. The character-building influence of personal example in nineteenth-century America is lacking in the twentieth. Parents who wish to transmit charitable and philanthropic attitudes to their children must structure their methods in the fulfillment of these aims. Parents who write the checks that support the voluntary organizations can call attention to the causes they are supporting, but children must be rather mature before they understand the check that Daddy signs represents dollars he has earned through diligent labor. Thoughtful, earnest parents desiring to transmit their own civic and humanitarian commitments and involvements to their children will be remarkably ineffectual if they limit themselves to verbal communications.

Sophisticated industrialists frequently plan open houses in their plants especially for the families of their employees. Although these programs are expensive, they are profitable in the long run. For children who understand and appreciate the work done by their parents to maintain the family's standard of living cause their parents less trouble, less worry, less anxiety, and therefore less absenteeism. The stability of the family life of the employees of an industrial organization is reflected in its profit and loss statement. In the same way, parents who take their children on visits to social organizations, museums, parks and governmental buildings are actually preparing them for personal participation in the work of social betterment. Early visits prepare the children for later membership in Boy Scouts of America, Girl Scouts, Campfire Girls, hospital Candystripers, and other similar work. Attitudes, latent action, must be imprinted early if the lives of young people are to be influenced by the ideals of the society in which they are growing up.

In spite of governmental support of essential agencies of social amelioration, Americans still enjoy supporting private, voluntary organizations even after they have become eligible for federal grants.

TWENTIETH-CENTURY PROBLEMS

Many of these organizations have survived the problems they were designed to solve. The discovery of a vaccine for polio made the work of a national foundation against the disease anachronistic. So the foundation changed its name and its purpose, continuing to raise funds to support research investigating the causes of birth defects and, where possible, to devise cures. Many of these organizations are characterized by networks of friendships that are meaningful and significant to those who have given them support in previous decades. But the interest of the parents in these organizations will not be maintained by their children when they attain to maturity unless their programs justify their continued existence. The involvement of young people and their integration into the program-planning apparatus is as important for the agencies as it is for the maintenance of traditional American ideals and moral concerns.

In most American communities, a considerable group of agencies have federated together for fund raising, planning, and programming. Some make collective purchases and undertake cooperative programs of educational training. Most of the community federations comprise organizations operating on the community level, but many have included national organizations as well. Philanthropic federations have a tendency to enlarge the picture of community organizations to such an extent that the individual may find it difficult to discover himself or his place in them. Federated giving is an essential part of the twentieth-century American society, enlarged, urbanized, and sophisticated in its technology, commerce, science, and industry. Unless the individual has some personal involvement with at least one of the federated agencies, it may become extremely difficult for him to understand how any of them operates. This is especially true of the young people who must be expected to assume these responsibilities in future decades.

Organizations originally religiously motivated generally continue to attract the support of their religious groups in the fund raising, personal service, education and training, study and research, or combinations of the same. The tendency of the communities to accept these services often deprives them of their sectarian identifications; they find themselves facing problems similar to those of secular organizations enjoying no denominational loyalty or support.

COMMUNITY PROBLEMS COVERED

Churches, synagogues, schools, and private families that want to transmit philanthropic values and civic ideals must offer their members opportunities for personal exposure to a wide variety of social services. While pictures are more instructive than words, actual participation is more effective than both. Visitations are effective, but actual sharing in the work of an agency, whenever possible, is preferable. A perusal of a community's directory of social services reveals problem areas with which the various branches of the social welfare apparatus are concerned: adoptions, aging, alcoholism, assistance to the needy, blindness, camps and other children's institutions, clinical problems including dental, medical, psychiatric, psychological, and other forms of rehabilitation, community centers, community planning and fund raising, day care centers for children, disaster service, employment problems, family and individual counseling, foster home placement, health services, homemaker service, hospitals, housing, mental health and retardation, migrants, probation and parole, protective services for children, recreation and group activities, servicemen and veterans, unmarried parents, vocational services, and volunteers. A directory of a community's mental health resources includes listing of outpatient mental hygiene clinics for children and adults, residential clinics and hospitals for children and adults, services for the mentally retarded, as well as professional services and organizations. All of these need public interpretation and most of them solicit public support, either financial or personal. Obviously no one individual, however highly motivated, could become personally involved in his community's entire program of social welfare. At the same time, religious and educational programs are incomplete if they do not include opportunities for both visitations and participation in activities for community betterment.

THE WORLD COMMUNITY

Americans are characteristically concerned with world problems, especially since World War II. Each of the major religious groups, Roman Catholic, Protestant, and Jewish, solicits support for overseas causes. Some of these are religiously motivated missions, but many are dedicated to human welfare without any evangelistic purposes, expressed or implied. There are also world-level organizations of a purely secular nature. Some of these have governmental support or endorsement. Modern transportation and communication have conspired to make our world smaller than it ever was before. Those who need to feel themselves "citizens of the world" welcome opportunities to support these undertakings, and young people especially want to participate in them actively. The Peace Corps attracts many of the American youths and enables them to share in the world's problems.

The United Nations represents mankind's historic hope for "One World." The United Nations organization is supported in this country by an association with chapters in every leading population center. Its humanitarian efforts and its cultural and economic programs are represented by UNICEF and UNESCO. In many communities, the celebration of Halloween is marked by the collection of pennies and other small coins by American children on a night ("Beggars' Night") that in other times would have found them going from door to door asking for "treats" they did not need and threatening "tricks" that could be as dangerous for them as they were often damaging to their neighbors. Many churches and synagogues participate in this program, teaching their pupils the meaning of world responsibility and concern for other children in the underprivileged nations of the world.

It is ironic that some people are not favorably disposed toward the ideal which has moved the hearts of men at least since the time of Isaiah. Many children have returned home from their door-to-door appeals on Beggars' Night with almost unbelievable stories of abuse poured out on them by those who oppose the whole idea of the United Nations, to say nothing of its auxiliaries. Parents have the task of interpreting such chauvinism to their children along with their explanations of the aims of the United Nations.

For those who seek involvement in the world in which they live, there are many—almost too many—causes to which they can commit themselves. Sincerely responsible people actually have to have a scale of values and a system of priorities by which they limit their activities for humankind if they are not to scatter their efforts in so many directions as to make them vain and meaningless. Those who prefer not to involve themselves in humanity's causes may find themselves strangers in a meaningless, indifferent world like that described by Albert Camus in *The Stranger*. His leading character lives through a meaningless childhood in the home of his parents, in the family of his orientation. Quite naturally, he finds himself in a world as absurd and nonsensical as that in which he was first socialized. The child who is privileged to grow up in a family whose horizons are cosmic will find himself in a world in which there is much to be done, problems to be solved, wrongs to be righted, and evils to be overcome, but never absurd or meaningless.

The dimensions of this problem are not merely personal; they are also cosmic. Since the beginning of the atomic era in 1945, the world's peril of self-destruction has been impending. Its tolerance of exaggerated patriotism has diminished rapidly, almost to the vanishing point. If the world does not destroy itself in a series of reciprocal nuclear explosions, its direction will have to be determined by men and women of goodwill whose concerns are universal. Enlightened love of country today demands an international point of view. The most critical shortage in the modern world is of people with a world view and a cosmic sense of human responsibility. Such personalities are to be developed mainly at home by families whose values embrace all humanity.

16

Your Friends And Leisure Activities

•

"Birds of a feather flock together," but human beings become
the kind of people their associations make them. To a very great
extent, personalities develop through human interaction; we become the kind of people our associations make us. Ironically, the
greatest perils seem to lurk in the unstructured hours of leisure
time; their number is increasing in a society whose affluence and
productivity have been vastly enhanced by scientific progress and
technological advance. Whenever weekends are lengthened by
the addition of a holiday, the number of accidental deaths and
homicides increases markedly. Juvenile delinquency and accident
rates increase annually during the summer months of traditional
school vacation. It is obvious that the American people find it
more difficult to cope with leisure time than with planned activity.

Since the beginning of the twentieth century, the regular working week in the United States has been reduced from sixty to
forty hours. Paid vacations are traditional, even for factory workers. Household appliances and labor-saving devices have greatly
reduced the time obligation of homemakers. American workers,
farmers, and homemakers have all joined the leisure class. Newcomers to the category seem to have more difficulty with it than
those whose parents and grandparents had leisure time at their
disposal. The number of these newcomers is far greater than that
of the veterans and the descendants of veterans in leisure-time

activities. Consequently, the need for education and training for the disposition of leisure time has become critical.

Again, the family is unexcelled and, in all probability, unequaled as a school for education and training for the profitable use of leisure. This function of the modern American family can no more be left to chance than the others. The family must have aims and goals for the disposition of its leisure time. Since no two family units are alike in this country, indeed, since individuality holds a sanctity accorded it nowhere else in the world, no one can tell a family what its aims and goals should be, and few families can successfully prescribe them for each of their members. However, it is important for each family to be aware of the probable consequences of leisure-time disposition so that their planning might ascribe higher priorities to the desired consequences and lower ones to the less desired and the not desired.

For example, a family with young children will want to plan activities in which they are included. Even after the children enter their adolescence, when they may become less willing to participate in family recreation, they will cherish the memories of family outings, picnics, and games. Even adolescents experience the residual joys of those experiences which they would not want to repeat during the period of their growth when association with parents reminds them that they have not yet achieved the maturity to which they pretend.

The abundance of commercial and other organized recreation opportunities for children away from parents and for parents without children offers great temptations to parents who want to spend their vacations away from their children. The adolescence of their children will afford them more time for this type of vacation. Before the adolescence of their children, however, wise parents usually give higher priority to leisure-time activities which include their offspring. Of course, all parents need to have some time that they can spend alone together, immune from demands of the social and economic structures.

Again, parents in the lower socioeconomic brackets generally have more children and less free time. Yet their need to get away from their children is much more critical than that of more comfortable middle-class parents. At the same time, children should have leisure-time activities with their parents before adolescence. Indeed, each child ought to have some experience alone with each parent; otherwise, it is difficult for children to have intimate views of the opposite-sex and same-sex parents in performance of their respective roles. Without such experiences, children mature with warped and distorted ideas of these roles and their meanings.

Psychiatrists and social scientists postulate that social malfunction is occurring with increasing frequency in our society because the adult roles are not imprinted firmly enough or frequently enough upon the minds of young children. Some argue that the phenomenon of homosexuality is increasing among American males because of the absence of the father from the home and the relative rarity of males on American school staffs. In any event, even children from two-parent homes may find themselves in difficulties when they are called upon to play adult roles in marriage and in families of their own establishment. Many of these difficulties arise from the infrequency of their childhood interactions with their parents.

At every level of the social structure, parents and children need to share leisure-time activities; at most levels, parents and children need leisure-time activities *away* from each other. In budgeting time together and apart from each other, parents of younger children can give priority to joint activities while parents of adolescent children should expect that few of their activities will be shared by both generations.

Americans are probably the most mobile people on earth. They love to travel. When travel was restricted during the two World Wars, the resentment of the average American was high. Currently, the distances traveled by Americans and the modes of their travel depend upon time and funds available to the family.

Obviously, travel with children is more expensive and therefore restricts the distances contemplated and the modes to be used.

Parents who are aware of the contents of the curricula of the schools and especially in the classes attended by their children will be able to plan trips that will be complementary to the work their children are doing in school. They can plan to visit historical places or parts of the country in which geological formations have been exposed by Nature herself as if she were preparing them for exhibition. Parents of young children may lack the time and the money for extensive travel by themselves, and children of affluent parents often express resentment against parents who send them away or leave them in the care of servants so that they can take trips abroad. The extensive travels of husbands and wives by themselves should be deferred until their children have at least attained to adolescence.

But this does not mean that husbands and wives cannot seek recreation together apart from their children. They can have dates even though they are married. They can revisit the scenes of their courtship and relive some of their premarital moments. While it might not be wise for them to leave young children for two weeks or a month, they should have a weekend now and then and an evening out more frequently.

The same principle applies to other activities which parents might share with their children or enjoy by themselves. Such recreational activities include listening to radio and watching television, making and enjoying music, reading silently or aloud, attending movies, parties, and sports events, playing games and dancing. Many parents and children make projects of visits to museums and art galleries. Obviously, taste will differ greatly between parents and young children; the priorities will be given to the preferences and the needs of young children, but the tastes and preferences of parents ought not to be entirely precluded. All of these activities may be indulged at various levels. Parents who enjoy drinking and gambling will probably not want to involve their young children in these activities. Moreover, preferences for drinking and gambling among husbands and wives do not correlate with marital happiness. They tend to be the preferences of either husband or wife rather than both.

Just as observer and spectator activities must be selected with respect to age variations, so, too, with participant activities; for example, many families enjoy playing golf or tennis together. Few families are large enough for a regulation game of baseball, basketball, or football. Male golfers might be willing to play with their wives and older children on appropriate occasions. In tennis, family foursomes are more common. Many parents have taught chess to their children only to discover that their pupils soon surpass them; the pupils eventually defeat their masters because they learned the game when they were younger.

INDOOR SPORTS

Billiards, Ping-Pong, and other table games are frequently enjoyed by whole families, regardless of age and sex.

The do-it-yourself movement has evoked such a popular response that doctoral dissertations have been written on various aspects of its impact upon American economic, social, and family life. The production of power tools and other similar equipment for home use has become a prosperous industry. Many families develop a sense of family cohesiveness, unity, and pride in their collective productivity. Some families will work together to make a closed-in sun-room out of a porch, or a screened-in porch out of an open one. Some families have built patios and formal gardens, others prefer to erect outdoor stoves for wiener and steak roasts. Some families redecorate their homes and even rebuild them in accordance with their changing needs.

Although collecting is usually an individual enterprise, it generally attracts the attention and favorable response of an entire family. It deserves to be classified as a family activity even though each member of the family might be collecting something else. Stamp and coin collectors of every age are all too willing to talk about their rare and fortunate finds. It is amazing how much history and geography are absorbed by the collectors and their families. Whole families are frequently interested in the collection of antiques. Little girls are more interested in doll collections than boys, but the latter frequently interest themselves furtively in their sisters' acquisitions. Both boys and girls share in the making of puppets and arranging puppet shows for their own amusement and for their guests.

One family known to the authors developed dramatic presentations for their own entertainment and for their friends. They began with simple representations of fairy tales and poems; their dramatic productions became more complex and more sophisticated with the passing of years.

Reading used to be an extremely popular family activity when books were rare and too expensive for large numbers of American families. A century ago, many American families owned only the Bible and no other book. Many Americans first heard the Bible read to them by their mothers; as many or more learned to read when they took their turns at reading the Bible to the family. The publishing industry discovered that specialization would increase profits. Books and magazines written and published specifically for boys or girls soon began to outsell adult literature. More recently, publishers discovered that costs could be reduced and profits increased by the publication of books and magazines that appeal to both boys and girls. "The Rover Boys" and "the Bobbsey Twins" have practically disappeared from the contemporary market. Children's books now have both male and female juvenile heroes with inevitable role confusion. The fantastic and the futuristic literatures are popular with the publishers because they are not circumscribed by cultural, geographical, social or ethnic boundaries. Parents sometimes find it difficult to follow their children into these far-out worlds of the imagination. The censorship of motion pictures and the designation of films for "adults" or "children" have affected American family life similarly. The same centrifugal forces that are profitable for publishers are also exploited by motion picture manufacturers and exhibitors. Nevertheless, some families read to each other, or share their reading experiences with each other. This practice and a similar sharing of motion picture and other entertainment are educational for the entire family and also contribute to domestic unity and cohesiveness.

Some families combine reading and travel. For instance, the authors used to do this on automobile trips when their children were young. Now that their offspring are grown parents, the authors have been gratified to discover that this practice has been continued by them; their grandchildren enjoy family reading on their automobile travels. In air-conditioned cars, with all windows closed, such reading programs are much more enjoyable than they formerly were. Such hobbies as reading together are unexcelled sources of motivation for leisure-time activity.

Musical families share an activity that can be meaningful to all regardless of age or sex. High-fidelity and stereophonic-sound families are more numerous than those who make their own music through their family orchestras or choruses. Some families collect commercial and privately made recordings; others make their own. The families who make their own music and do their own recording are more rare, but their combined hobbies keep them all busy regardless of the limitations of the talents or creativity of individual members. Dancing is associated with music, of course, in many families.

Many families are devoted to other arts. Oil on canvas and sculpture have their familial devotees. A midwestern clergyman induced his family to take up weaving. Individual members had private projects, but the family had a larger loom in their living room. On it they were weaving a rug according to a design which they borrowed from the public library. Even visitors in the household were frequently induced to share in weaving the rug the family was making. Of all the arts, photography is certainly the most popular. Even during the dire phases of the American depression, photography fans had to have film. No other art stimulates extraversion and interest in others to the extent that photography does. The photographer is always looking for subjects; he sees things that other people miss and discovers beauty in scenes and people that others take for granted. Whether he shows his pictures on screens or by passing them around, his highest reward is the approval of others. Rabid photography fans insist on having their own darkrooms even when they live in high-rise apartment houses. The larger the part they play in the production of their pictures, the prouder they are and the more willing they are to discuss photography with other addicts.

COMMUNICATIONS

Perhaps the most extraverting of all of the family hobbies are the communications undertakings. Ham radio operators find themselves communicating with other hobbyists all over the country and sometimes all over the world. The amateur radio expert is really part of a world family. Amateurs communicate with each other at mutually convenient times; these hours are rarely conventional. The wireless apparatus or radio telephone may be located in the home of the licensed amateur operator, but it becomes the medium through which friendships are established across national, racial, and religious boundaries. Periodically, the hams meet in conventions to give reality to their ethereal friendships.

Pen pals can develop similar relationships without elaborate electronic equipment; they need stationery and postage, and little else. Sometimes pen pals exchange gifts, but customs regulations frequently impose difficulties. Structured meetings of pen pals are less common than radio amateurs' gatherings, but pen pals do meet each other personally on occasions, either accidentally or through carefully devised plans. Students of foreign languages in different countries strengthen their commands of the languages they are studying through the exchange of letters with peers in lands in which those languages are spoken. Visits to those countries become particularly meaningful when the pen pals can look forward to their personal meetings.

GARDENING

Rural children are no strangers to the miracle of growth. The children of farmers frequently share in the agricultural enterprise; most of them have sections of their own for which they have been induced to feel responsible. Urban children ought to have similar opportunities. This is not easy when families live in apartment houses, but even then, flowers and some vegetables can be grown in window boxes. Shortly after the beginning of their marriage, the authors lived in a small apartment. They had been told that the top of a sweet potato could be planted in a Mason jar. There was a fine growth of green from that sweet potato.

When they became parents, the authors recommended such projects to their own children with similar results. Their own gratification was surpassed by their children's. Similar experiments in growth can be tried with other vegetables and even flowers. The children of families who dwell in homes surrounded by some land should be encouraged to share with each other and with their parents in the care of the grounds and, if possible, they could have small patches of the land assigned to them for their own cultivation. It is very difficult for urban children to confront reality independently and without adult supervision and direction; gardening is an activity in which people come face to face with the miracle of growth. One wise old Jewish mother told her son that the seeds she gave him for planting would enable him to enter into a "partnership with God." This introduction to gardening gave him a hobby to follow all during the active years of his career, and after his retirement he was able to make a major preoccupation of it. In spite of cardiac difficulties diagnosed by his physician, he was encouraged to continue his gardening. His physician assured him that this activity would not be too strenuous for him but would give him productive and satisfying activity.

INDUSTRY AND PUBLIC SERVICE

Another technique which the authors have lived to see reproduced in the families of their offspring involved visitations to industrial plants and public service centers. Visits to airports, bus depots, and railroad stations were natural replies to the inquiries of the children with respect to travel and transportation. On a Sunday afternoon one of the authors was the speaker at a sorority house function. The care of the children was left to her husband for the afternoon. He took them for a visit to the railroad station, a "first" experience for all of them since their experience with travel had been almost exclusively by air and by automobile. When the father explained his purpose to the yardmaster, he was obviously interested and not a little flattered. He offered the children a ride on one of the engines used in the yard. You can imagine how excited they were when they had a chance to tell their mother about their experiences that afternoon!

When the children were puzzled about the dial telephone and the remarkable way in which they could reach their friends by dialing the appropriate numerals, their parents took them on a tour of the telephone company. The response of one of the representatives of management was most enthusiastic; he conducted the parents and their children on a tour of the building and explained the way in which modern telephones work.

The children were similarly interested in motorcars, automobile tires, and hot dogs. These inquiries resulted in visits to an automobile factory, a tire factory, and a sausage factory. More recently the authors listened to the enthusiastic reports of their grandchildren whose inquiries had been answered in similar ways.

The authors also took their children to visit a fire station house, a police station, and even the county jail. These visits gave the children a clear idea of the service offered the community by these units. The policemen, firemen, and sheriff were most willing to explain their facilities and to answer the questions put to them by the children. When the children were in high school, they visited local courts ranging from the municipal magistrates' courts to the Federal District Court. Another interesting visit required sixty miles of travel to the state capitol, where the legislature was in session. Like many other parents, the present authors took their children on a trip to Washington, D.C., during which they toured the nation's Capitol under competent guidance.

All of these are opportunities for confrontations with reality, but none of them excels the acquisition of the skills learned at home through carpentry, electrical and plumbing work, cooking, sewing, and other similar forms of family activity.

17

Your Religious Faith

•

WHEN LAYMEN ENGAGE IN RELIGIOUS DISCUSSIONS, they frequently confront difficulties in terminology. Especially when they represent the majority groups in a particular locality, Christians usually find themselves discussing or arguing theological and philosophical beliefs and views. Interdenominational disputes generally concern ideological differences. When Jewish laymen question Christians about their religion, their queries generally concern Christian practices and ritual observances even though they frequently ask about such doctrines as the Virgin birth, the Resurrection, and Original Sin. Because of these variations in emphasis, dialogues between laymen are frequently frustrating to the participants. Rabbis, priests, and ministers participate in these discussions more fruitfully because they are aware of the categories of their discussion and generally try not to violate them.

So it is found that Jews will answer the question "Why should I join a synagogue?" with some such reply as: "It is a good place to become acquainted and to meet people." If they have a choice, they would prefer to join a synagogue whose rituals and practices are more similar to those of their preference and previous experience. To the question "Should I join a church?" the prospective Christian usually attempts a theological or philosophical answer. As the community grows in number and expands in size, both Christians and Jews are frequently influenced by proximity in their selection of a church or synagogue. All other things being equal, they generally prefer the church or synagogue that is not too distant from them.

Religion functions in family life, as in all human interaction, when all three of its essential elements are operative: 1) social, 2) methodological, and theologico-philosophical. When religion is being discussed, it may not be possible to give full consideration to all three at one and the same time. When the social aspects of religion are under discussion, the discussants are really delving into the sociology of religion. As long as they know that they are limiting themselves to one category, the discussion can be fruitful. Considerations of religious methodology are the appropriate concern of the psychologists of religion, and the theological and philosophical aspects of religion are within the province of the theologian and the philosopher. The evaluation of religion or religions is on safe ground as long as the categories are maintained for purposes of discussion and there is full recognition of the fact that no one of them constitutes the totality of religion. All three are part of functioning religion.

When a religious organization is regarded merely as another social institution, its effectiveness in terms of life is diminished. When the method of expression is treated as if it were the essence of religion, that religion is reduced to an empty formalism. Without embodiment in a social group following a method of religious expression, neither theology nor philosophy can function as religion does in the lives of people. No religion can be completely effective without each of these essential elements.

Individuals or families may become affiliated with a particular church or synagogue because of their preference for the social group of which it is constituted, its ritual, its preaching, or its music, or its theological and philosophical approach. Even though the affiliation is established because of one aspect of the religious organization or another, the impact of the religion upon that person or family is holistic if the religion is functioning properly. There is a saying in the Talmud: "Although he comes for a partial purpose, he leaves with a total effect." Although a person may be attracted to a church or synagogue by its preacher, the religion represented by that institution will not actually function in his life until he becomes an active member of the organization expressing its religious point of view in daily life through action whether real or symbolic but preferably both.

Although individuals generally feel that religion is an intensely personal experience, it is actually a social phenomenon. This is what Rabbi Hillel meant when he said: "Separate not thyself from the congregation; trust not in thyself until the day of thy death; pass not judgment upon thy neighbor until thou art come into his place; and do not say, 'when I have leisure I will study'; thou mayest never have the leisure." The person to whom the church or synagogue is nothing more than a means of socialization is not likely to experience the full impact of the religion taught there, just as the one who devotes himself entirely to pious rituals or theological and philosophical discussions can hardly be called religious.

Some people, especially youth, are actually alienated from religion by experiences with churches or synagogues in which the emphasis is upon one or another of the essential elements of religion with real or apparent disregard for the others. Many young people and others cannot believe the required creed of a particular religious organization. Where the principal emphasis is creedal, and identification is made between creed and religion in common parlance, such persons feel excluded. They go from denomination to denomination hopelessly and endlessly searching for a creed they can accept. For a thinking person, this is very difficult; what he firmly believes in one phase of his life he may completely outgrow by the next. The youth who grows up believing that a full and complete relationship with God is maintained through persistent and unfailing regularity in ritual practice may find himself denying religion altogether because of the obvious ineffectiveness of these practices by themselves regardless of the diligence of his pious observances. Those who think of the church or the synagogue merely as opportunities for socialization will soon discover that their place in his life can easily be filled by clubs, fraternities, or sororities.

It is not uncommon for a young person to return home from college on his first vacation with the announcement to his family that he will never again accompany them to their church or their synagogue or participate with them in their family worship. He will make a flamboyant and grandiloquent reference to a philosophy class or a science laboratory to explain his loss of faith. His parents might say that he lost his religion at the university, but he probably never had religion in the first place! He may have had a creed which was discredited by a classroom lecture or discussion or demonstration. That was all he lost. A young man might come home after the fulfillment of his military obligation and disclose to his unhappy parents that he no longer observes his religion. "While I was in the Army," he explains, "I couldn't put on my *tefilin* (phylacteries) to say my morning prayers, nor could I eat *kosher*. I learned how to get along without religion and now I have lost it altogether." In actuality, Judaism is much more than the rituals by which it is expressed. The same is true of every other valid religion. The former soldier may have lost certain habits, certain obsessive, compulsive behavior patterns during his military experience, but he could not have lost a religion which he obviously never had!

Currently, young people express dissatisfaction with church or synagogue youth programs that are not relevant to the world in which they live. Most young people today are painfully conscious of social problems, inequities and injustices. They want their church or synagogue to suggest a program of social action; mere socialization is hardly enough for them. At the same time, it must be recognized that the church and synagogue must continue to be social organizations; they must also have techniques, such as rituals and liturgies, for the transmission of their abiding values. Religious institutions cannot survive as purely social reform agitation centers. Nor can churches or synagogues survive the current social revolution if they do not take a proper part in it, offering effective leadership in accordance with their professed value systems.

RELIGION BEGINS AT HOME

It is highly improbable that children coming from families without any religious identification will feel at home in a church or a synagogue. It is even less likely that children whose experience with religion at home has been negative will be open-minded with respect to religion: they will be "blocked" against religion in most cases. Parents can prepare their children for ritual experiences by motivating them through home practices clearly indicating or symbolizing religious interest. If religious strictures, inhibitions, or mandates are imposed upon children by parents who are not personally involved with religious activity, the children may accept the imposed norms and commands until they understand that their parents do not accept them for themselves.

We have frequently observed expressions of resentment by children of parents who insist that they must go to Sunday school, religious school, or Hebrew school even though they themselves rarely or never attend church or synagogue or any facility offered by a religious institution for adult education. We have also observed the negative consequences of role reversals in Jewish families. Many pre-schools sponsored by Jews and other Jewish religious schools have used children as a means of influencing parents in the direction of religious observances. Some synagogues send Sabbath candles, prayers, and candlesticks home with the children to persuade their parents to have the Sabbath home observance. Parents are usually gratified by this influence of the pre-school or synagogue school upon their children. As long as the children insist, the parents maintain home observances, and frequently boast of the fact that their children taught them Judaism. Subsequently, these parents may be amazed when their children rebel against all religion. They fail to understand that when the children were younger, the role reversal caused them to clearly identify religious practice with childhood and interpret adulthood as the time in which one is excused from the requirements of religious practice. Such children often interpret Bar Mitzvah, Bas Mitzvah, or Confirmation as "graduation from religion." The parents are enthusiastic about the pre-school or other elementary education that prompted the children to teach Judaism to their parents. At the same time, they erroneously blame the post-Confirmation class or youth program of the congregation or community center for the alienation of their children.

In both Judaism and Christianity the proper parental role is that of the teacher of religion. No institution or institutional functionary can take the place of the parent as the teacher of religious values. At best, the institution and its agents can augment the instruction of parents. They can build upon foundations laid by the parents. It is very unusual for children who have been the teachers of their parents in the field of religion to have respect for their parents during middle or late adolescence.

Prayers at mealtimes, before bedtime, and after waking up in the morning are among the most effective means that parents can use to imprint their young children with a motivation for religion that will function in childhood and continue on through adolescence and adult life. Parents who tell or read Bible stories to their children will undoubtedly find that those children are more favorably disposed to Bible stories when they attend a religious school and that they will be much more interested in the sermons of the priest, minister, or rabbi when they attend church or synagogue services. Buying recorded Bible stories may be a way in which parents think that their place can be taken by a more dramatic narrator, but no machine can take the place of a live and personally involved parent.

Christian parents who allow Christmas to become completely commercialized should not be surprised if it subsequently loses all spiritual meaning for their children, if they see it merely as a season for fun and good times. Jewish parents who permit commercialization to secularize such holidays as Hanukkah, Purim, or Passover should not be surprised if the materialistic aspects of these observances soon obscure the spiritual implications for their children. Parents who are really concerned about the religious motivation of their children can resist commercialization of religion by creativity, originality, and personal involvement.

Parents who attend classes and worship services at their own churches or synagogues will find that their children are much less resentful of their insistence upon attendance at Sunday school, religious school or Hebrew school than those children whose parents fretfully or fitfully take them to the church or synagogue and "dump them off," expecting the religious institution to "gas them up," supply them with religious fuel for the remainder of the week. The authors have been more amused than amazed by parents whose attendance at worship services is infrequent but whose complaints against their children for their indifference to religion are constant. What is wrong with their children? Sometimes they ask, "What is the matter with the religious school?" Parents who are themselves committed to religious activity and observance and who enforce it upon their children so strictly that it becomes a barrier between them and their peers will also find that the compulsion will be resented and frequently resisted by the children.

One of the most important functions of religious observance in the home is the formalized expression of affection. The Jewish children who witness the blessing of the candles Sabbath after

Sabbath know that their mother is praying for them. Their father's recitation or chanting of Kiddush over the wine and the bread is equally affectional. But children are sensitive receivers of feelings their parents might not realize they are broadcasting. Those who love transmit love in their religious observances at home. Those who fear transmit fear. Those who hate transmit hostility. Religious home observances are excellent media of communication for genuine and sincerely felt affection. Adults may be fooled by counterfeit religious expression, but not children!

Parents who prepare the Passover Seder at home will discover that it will mean more and its influence will be more enduring upon their children than a community Seder prepared and offered by the local synagogue or Jewish community center. This principle applies to religion in general: ritual observance within the family has the most powerful impact on each participant regardless of age.

The completeness, soundness, welfare, and peace of the individual is the function of religion, but that is not all! The integration of the individual in society and its completeness, soundness, welfare, and peace is a proper function of religion, but that is not all! The integration of all societies in the world with each other and, of course, the individuals within each constitutes the *ultimate* goal of religion. Thus, in the immediate sense, the word includes many conflicts; in the *ultimate* sense, ideally all these conflicts are resolved. The aim of religion is to enable the individual to accept himself at the same time that he accepts his appropriate place in his social groups and, indeed, in the world of which he is a part. The methods and techniques of religion should add up to the unification of the individual and the totality: mankind.

Because religions differ from each other, and even more because each individual is or ought to be a unique personality, it is impossible to propose any perfect, universal program for the achievement of wholeness (SHALOM). Each family and each individual must make its own decisions on the basis of its own religious heritage and unique experience. With the guidance and direction of his or her own pastor, priest, or rabbi, each individual will have to work out a program of religious expression that satisfies his needs at the same time as he hopes to achieve a complete identification with society and the world.

PART V

•

SOME SPECIAL PROBLEMS

18

Childlessness

●

THOMAS J. REESE

Thomas J. Reese, a Monsignor of the Diocese of Wilming-
ton, Delaware, is the Director of Catholic Social Services, Inc., Wil-
mington. Trained in theology and social work at the Catholic University of America, he has worked at the Child Center of Catholic
University. He is a member of and has held offices in many social
organizations and associations: National Association of Social Workers, Community Services Council, National Catholic Social Action
Conference, Family Court Association of Delaware, Child Welfare
League of America, Delaware Inter-Agency Committee on Adoption,
National Council on Family Relations, National Social Welfare As-
sembly, and others. He has also written widely in professional jour-
nals and popular magazines.

●

WHEN A COUPLE MARRY, they make a basic commitment and investment in each other. Their friendship and love, their generous
giving, should be a source of fulfillment, satisfaction, and growth
to each of them.

The old song reminds us that love and marriage go together.
In the minds of most couples, children and marriage do, too.
Producing and rearing children is very much in the minds of
most couples contemplating marriage, and some talk about it in

great detail, sharing their convictions on the subject and, thereby, learning to know each other better.

Many young couples' attitude toward having children is like that of St. Augustine's toward purity: "O Lord, make me chaste— but not yet." Because of the trend to earlier marriages and the lengthened period involved in preparation for gainful employment, it is sometimes inadvisable to have children immediately, and many couples plan to postpone their family.

Reasons why people want children vary widely. Often the couple themselves haven't thought the matter through. Children are an important status symbol, and the childless spouse can quickly feel inferior when surrounded by peers chattering about the latest cute sayings and achievements of their offspring.

For some, children are a projection of themselves, an incarnation of their mutual love, an assurance of a kind of family immortality. It is not surprising that some of our larger families are composed of a series of girls as the parents keep trying for a son. More often in the past, but even today, some couples simply accept children as the natural outcome of marriage and the sexual relationship. Some even consider it the price they pay for having a little fun.

Most religious traditions strongly emphasize children as a blessing, and their marriage liturgy reflects this. When children don't arrive, the childless couple often wonder if they are out of favor with God.

Finally, there are couples who thoroughly enjoy parenthood because of the challenges they find in rearing children. They like to see the child grow and develop and obtain great satisfaction from being part of the process and making their contribution.

In bygone centuries, children were often an economic asset, providing income and security for parents. In today's world this is rarely true. The rearing of children is an expensive and prolonged process.

Children add a dimension to marriage that can enhance even the most satisfying husband-wife relationship. As time passes, many couples find a trace of boredom creeping into their life. While they love each other, they begin getting a little tired of each other. Mannerisms become irritating. The intense preoccupation with each other begins to pall. Conception, pregnancy, birth, and parenthood modify their relationship and give them an additional focus, an occasion for deeper understanding of each other and an opportunity to work together in loving and serving someone beyond themselves.

As time passes and conception does not take place, most couples start to become concerned. They begin trying harder to make a baby, and for some it becomes almost an obsession. Intercourse is timed to occur at a period of greatest fertility. Rather than being a means of expressing affection, it becomes an occasion for a performance. Tensions mount.

I knew one couple who had been going through this for years. When they finally decided to apply for adoption, they were such nervous wrecks that the agency referred them to a psychiatrist to help them get unwound.

Medical aspects of infertility have changed dramatically in the past several years. It used to be estimated that one couple in ten could not have children of their own. Increased knowledge of physiology, more sophisticated surgical procedures, and the use of hormones have reduced this proportion so that many couples of borderline fertility can now be parents.

When children do not come, most couples turn to their doctor for assistance. Often the cause of sterility is determined, and sometimes it can be corrected. Curiously, there are many instances in which, even after a thorough medical workup, no cause of childlessness can be discovered. These are the couples who, after they decide to apply for adoption, in the course of their study or after their approval as adoptive parents suddenly become pregnant. The experience of any adoption agency will testify that such cases are not uncommon. There are many cases also in which, after several years of childlessness, the couple adopt and then go on to have natural children of their own.

The causes of this phenomenon are not clear, but in all likelihood the couple have tried too hard and developed anxieties and tensions that interfered with their endocrine system. Perhaps some unconsciously fear the responsibilities of parenthood and doubt their ability to meet them. When a child has actually been placed with them and they find they can function well as parents, or when they receive indication from an agency in which they have confidence that they have been accepted as adoptive parents, their anxiety is dispelled, and their body can function more efficiently. This whole question would make an interesting research project.

In some instances the likelihood of being unable to produce children is known prior to marriage. In all fairness, it should be shared with one's intended spouse, lest he feel tricked or cheated later on. More often than not, there are no indications of infertility prior to marriage, and when children are not forthcoming, the couple seek medical assistance. Generally it is the wife who takes the initiative and undergoes tests first. This is understandable since the reproductive mechanism of the female is somewhat more complicated and has both the possibilities of more going wrong and the likelihood of corrective measures being successful. Often, too, the wife's taking the initiative in having herself examined reflects a consideration for her husband and the kinds of feelings many men have regarding their infertility. Since the husband is also involved, he can save his wife some of the more complicated diagnostic tests by submitting to tests himself. For a husband to permit his wife to submit herself to these extreme measures without undergoing even routine infertility studies himself is most inconsiderate.

The whole question of sterility can be highly charged emotionally. Consciously or unconsciously, many men equate their fertility with their masculinity and feel less a man if they are sterile. Some men won't even permit themselves to find out and resist any kind of exploration. A man so insecure that he can't face himself for what he is would likely be handicapped in relating to his wife and adopted children.

Infertility is also a threat to women. Even when they are obviously well endowed with feminine characteristics, their inability to bear a child can be a source of extreme disappointment and affect their concept of themselves as women and as mothers. Biological motherhood is no guarantee that a woman can perform the maternal role, nor is the fact that a woman cannot bear a child any indication that she is unable to mother a child.

Sometimes the emotional trauma surrounding sterility is so great that it seriously affects the spouse's image of himself and distorts the relationship to his partner. Some of this frequently comes out in the course of adoption studies, and the couple are helped to work it through. In extreme instances, psychiatric help is indicated.

If the couple are mature and have basically a good relationship to each other, the fact of sterility can present an additional opportunity for them to show their understanding and love. However, if their basic relationship is not good, sterility can become a cause for recrimination and convert their relationship into a power struggle. Poorly informed piety causes some couples to abstain from marital relations if conception is not possible. This can create tensions that may eventually destroy the marriage.

Many childless couples never come to adoption. Others do within a few years after marriage. Some who know their infertility apply within a few months after marriage. This creates a problem for the adoption agency because they want to make sure the couple have had time to get adjusted to each other and establish the kind of relationship that parenthood requires.

Even when it has become clear that adoption is the only way to a family, many couples find the decision hard to make. They know of the risk and uncertainty involved in black and gray market adoptions. Licensed adoption agencies tend to have a poor image because they are often pilloried in the press, especially in the slick women's magazines. Their procedures, intended to protect the child and adopting couple, are seen as unnecessary red tape, and the adoption study—which is necessary to enable the agency to know the couple, evaluate their potential parenthood, and make a decision as to the kind of child who would best fit into their family—is viewed as an invasion of privacy.

In addition, there are still some fears about "bad seed." Most children placed in adoption are born of women out of wedlock. Feelings about illegitimacy come into play. Friends and relatives can cause embarrassment, too. Relatives, especially, may have a negative attitude toward bringing into the family someone not of the same blood.

Complicating the whole picture may be a sense of guilt, wondering whether God is punishing one for some real or imagined sin of the past. There is also the fear of being rejected by the agency. At one time, most adoption agencies had many more applicants than they had children available. Some of them set up requirements based not so much on sound professional principles or even common sense as the need to screen out the applicants and get their number down to manageable size. This is no longer true in most agencies. In some parts of the country, the number of children available for adoption placement is actually greater than the number of applicants. This results from the improvement in infertility work and the steady increase in the number of illegitimate children.

In most agencies, the waiting time and the time required to do the study has steadily decreased to a point where many agencies routinely beat the stork by placing a child in adoption in less than nine months from initial inquiry.

The adoption study itself can and should be a constructive experience for the couple. While certain information is necessary, it is not primarily an "investigation," but a process in which the agency comes to know the couple and the couple come to know and understand each other better. In a sense, the study is a school in parenting and helps the couple prepare to be parents. It serves somewhat the same purpose as nine months of pregnancy, but there is no need for it to be so painful as giving birth.

The criteria used by most agencies in deciding whether to place a child for adoption with a couple are basically the same as most couples would use if, knowing their death was imminent and having no close friends or relatives, they had to decide from several applicants which couple they would choose as parents for their child.

They would want to know if the spouses were mature, reasonably well adjusted, and emotionally and physically fit. They would want to know what kind of attitudes and values they had and what they would impart to a child in terms of character, training, and development. They would want to know how the couple viewed a child, whether they could tolerate a child and be flexible enough to meet the child's needs in his varying stages of development. They would want the couple to have a reasonable life expectancy and the ability to provide shelter, food, and the other physical needs of a child. Most would want to know the couple's religious commitment and practice and the spiritual component in their lives.

Following the placement of a child, most states require a period of supervision by the agency or the courts. "Supervision" does not connote investigation or spying. Rather, it is a period when the professional resources of the agency are at the disposal of the couple in the early months of adjustment to parenthood. It can be a constructive and helpful experience, and it usually is.

When the required supervisory period is over, the couple make their final decision as to having the child as their own, and the agency gives its consent. A formal petition is presented to the appropriate court, and if in the opinion of the judge the plan is a good one for the child, he issues a decree of adoption. This makes the child in every respect the child of the adopting couple, just as though he had been theirs by birth. He is their full responsibility, and they have full parental rights.

Most childless couples come to adoption as a way of having a family. Generally they want infants, as young as possible. Many request "direct placements," which means the child comes to them directly from the hospital nursery without having been in foster care. The risk is slightly greater in such placements, but the psychological benefits to adoptive parents and child usually offset the risk.

As a rule of thumb, the older the child is the harder he is to place; although occasionally, because of age or other considerations, a couple will prefer an older child. Some couples also are very pragmatic about the whole matter. They would just as soon have one that didn't require a two o'clock feeding, or one that could walk, or, perhaps, one that was housebroken.

Some couples, and this is especially true of those who have already adopted children, come to see adoption as a way of serving children. This concept has been popularized and stressed, especially by Pearl Buck who has written movingly of the needs of "hard to place children" and has been instrumental in finding homes for many of them. Hard to place children include older children, handicapped children, and those of mixed or minority race.

Older children are a challenge because, usually, they have been through traumatic experiences that resulted in their not having a family of their own. Some are children who have lived in foster care—occasionally, in several foster homes. They require patience and understanding to dispel the suspicion and insecurity that they frequently have. They are likely to test out the adopting couple to be sure that they are loved for themselves. Sometimes these placements don't work out, and when this is apparent in the course of the supervisory year, plans can be made for the child's return. In a surprising number of instances, however, older children do adjust. It is a little harder and takes a little longer, but with understanding parents they can make it.

Handicapped children are usually hard to place. Handicaps can range the gamut from a weak eye muscle that makes a child appear cross-eyed but which can be corrected in time, to blindness or deafness or mental retardation or emotional instability. Usually, on their first or second go-around, a couple find it difficult to consider handicapped children, but on the third or fourth, they are often willing to try.

At times, couples who have had natural children and have considered themselves blessed by the health and happiness of their children consider adopting a handicapped child as a way of showing their gratitude and sharing their blessings. Usually, the agency has had expert diagnostic and therapeutic help, and the nature of a child's handicap is thoroughly understood. This is shared completely with the adoptive couple, as well as with the physician or other specialists who will be working with the child. Some agencies have actually developed contracts with adoptive couples whereby the agency agrees to underwrite unusual expense related to the handicap in question. In some instances this provides security for the couple and makes it possible for them to proceed with the adoption. It also provides a real home to a child who otherwise would not have one.

Minority or mixed-race children constitute a growing problem. Most experts who have studied illegitimacy agree that the unwed mother usually has deep psychological reasons for getting pregnant out of wedlock. Commonly, it is to punish her parents. In some instances it is a greater punishment if the child she produces is of mixed race. In any event, most child-caring agencies are finding that there is an increase in the number of such children coming under their care. These fine, healthy children didn't ask to be born, and society has just as much responsibility to provide for them as for the cute little blue-eyed blondes.

Most mixed-racial children in agency care are born of white mothers, since Negro and other minority group mothers tend to keep their babies. With the growing nationalism and black awareness in the Negro community, some childless Negro couples, who would have preferred or at least would have considered a mixed-racial child, are now insisting on a full Negro child in preference to one of mixed race. In an effort to provide for the mixed-racial child, a number of agencies are conducting campaigns in the white community to call the plight of these children to the attention of people of goodwill. Some couples who would like to take one of these children hesitate because of the expected reaction of neighbors and relatives and because they realize that, even as members of a white family, the dark-skinned youngsters will face discrimination as they grow up. Nevertheless some enlightened souls, despite the social pressure, have found it possible to open their homes and hearts and practice the kind of love spoken of by Christ and the Hebrew prophets.

A few childless couples who want children in their home consider foster care. Since foster care tends to be temporary, it is usually not a satisfactory solution for couples who want a child on a permanent basis. Most childless couples who want children want them permanently and as their very own. Foster care can seldom promise this.

Many children are in foster care as young infants, waiting to move into their adoptive homes. Others come under care of various ages because of family breakdown or crisis and look forward, eventually, to returning to their own homes. Such children are not usually legally free for adoption; although if the family situation is sufficiently acute, they might be freed through court action. There are times when an agency is reasonably sure that a child will need long-term foster care and can provide assurance to foster parents, but there is nearly always the possibility that some change in circumstances could result in the child's removal from the home.

A few young couples, while they are waiting for their own family to start, apply to do foster care, thinking that it will give them some experience and training in parenthood that will be helpful to them later on. Even in these instances, there is danger of a couple becoming overly attached to a child and having a very difficult time when the child has to move on.

There are a few childless couples who have been able to do foster care successfully and find great fulfillment and satisfaction from it. They have been pleased to see the progress and development of children who lived in their home and have not had the need to keep them permanently as their own. These are exceptional couples. They are almost like nurserymen who are satisfied to tend seedlings and young plants and happy to see them move on to a permanent place in someone else's garden.

For the average childless couple, foster care is likely to be a traumatic experience. However, there are exceptions, and some childless couples can do it.

Understandably, most couples who do foster care have children of their own. Sometimes, even when their children are young, they can find room for one more. More often, it is when the youngest child has started to school that they consider doing foster care. Foster homes are needed in almost every part of the country. A good foster home experience can sometimes change the course of a child's life. Undoubtedly, opening one's home and one's heart to a child who needs them is the ultimate form of personal and religious service.

There are other ways of filling the void of childlessness and serving children.

Childless couples can have a lot of fun and be a real help to their friends by doing some baby-sitting. Some of these experiences may even restore their faith in childlessness or at least make them realize that children are not an unmixed blessing.

Childless couples usually have more time to devote to community service. Many have found satisfaction and proved invaluable as adult leaders in various youth programs, den mothers, scoutmasters, and in a host of other roles.

On a broader basis, they can contribute their time and talents as board members and volunteers to the many children's case-work and group-work programs in their community.

When a couple have no children, the wife is likely to work, since the care of the home does not consume all her time and energy. Working on the staff of an agency or organization dealing with children, being a social worker, teacher, nurse, an attendant, or baby-sitter, provides an opportunity for serving children and brings a sense of fulfillment.

Parenthetically, spinsters and bachelors have an even greater problem. At least the married couples have each other, but, through various programs of service, many a bachelor and spinster have remained alive by working with children and are much more vital than married couples who have isolated themselves from children.

Having more time at their disposal, childless couples can serve children and the cause of good family life by engaging in pro-grams of social action, including politics. Too often, parents are so involved with the nitty-gritty problems they and their children have that they don't even think about the causes of these problems. Perhaps people who are more removed can concentrate more on causes and help change the system that produces the problems. Better laws might make better families and children.

Childlessness is not a punishment; it can sometimes be a bless-ing. Some husbands and wives are so wrapped up in their pro-fessions, their jobs, or their hobbies that, while they can give a great deal to each other, they have nothing left to give to children. Parents *are* necessarily tied down in serving their children. In many ways, childless couples can serve children more broadly than parents can.

Childless couples can help to demonstrate that a family is, first, a couple—that parenting is part of marriage but not all of it.

Earlier marriages and the longer life-span means that even couples with children now spend a greater part of their married life as couples. When their children have grown and gone, they may need help in rediscovering each other.

Ultimately, not having children can be a special problem in marriage. But having them can be, too. Who can say which is the greater problem? Doesn't it depend on what they do about it?

19

Ill Health and Disability

•

HOWARD J. CLINEBELL, JR.

Howard J. Clinebell is one of the leading spirits in the whole movement to enlarge and improve religious awareness of the human potential. Trained in the clinical aspects of pastoral care, he is now Professor of Pastoral Counseling at the School of Theology, Claremont, Calif. His writings include *Understanding and Counseling the Alcoholic, Mental Health Through the Christian Community*, and *Basic Types of Pastoral Counseling*. He is one of the founders of The American Association of Pastoral Counselors and served as its first President.

•

"THE TROUBLE SEEMED TO BEGIN when Jim was in the hospital and then was unable to work for three months after his accident. Something happened between us that hasn't healed along with his broken leg." This is how Karen Knudsen described the beginning of their marital problems to their pastor. Apparently the stresses following Jim's accident had precipitated a chain reaction of marriage conflicts.

THE NATURE OF A CRISIS

The capacity to handle crises constructively is essential to a growing marriage. What is a crisis? It is a person's response to any

198

situation which threatens or cuts off a major source of need satisfaction and which cannot be handled with his usual coping skills. The lost or threatened satisfactions can be physical (food, sex, etc.), psychological (love, esteem, security, belonging, etc.), or spiritual (a meaningful faith, purpose in life, relationship with God). A crisis happens *within* people and their relationships, not *to* them. It is a state of psychological disturbance, with feelings such as anxiety, inadequacy, confusion, anger and panic, often precipitated by external problems but caused by the inadequacy of old ways of satisfying one's needs and the difficulties of learning effective new ways. Crises are like forks in the road of mental health. If persons learn new, efficient coping skills, they strengthen their problem-handling resources and are better equipped for dealing with future challenges. Conversely, if they retreat from struggling with the problem and conquering it, their personality resources are weakened for future crises. Thus, crises are opportunities for either growth or regression.

This approach to crises, based on research in psychiatry, is useful in understanding and handling crises in family relationships. The Knudsens have a crisis in their marital interaction. Jim's disability aroused feelings of fear, anger, guilt and dependence in him, and equally intense, conflicted feelings in Karen. As they interacted, the feelings of each reinforced those of the other. Because their ability to communicate was limited, they were unable to resolve their hang-ups through open dialogue. The wall that grew between them further blocked their communication, stifling the two-way flow of foods of the spirit—love, companionship, esteem, nurture. Jim's disability also cut off sexual satisfaction and economic security, which compounded their relationship problems.

If, through pastoral counseling, the Knudsens learn effective ways of communicating, resolving conflicts, and dealing with feelings, they will be able to handle their practical problems. Furthermore, their marriage will be strengthened and vitalized by their new skills. If they fail, their wall will become an increasing barrier; their lack of "cope-ability" will continue to plague their marriage. Marriages which grow over the years are those in which sharing and overcoming painful problems have deepened the relationships and heightened the contrasting experiences of joyful sharing. One twenty-years-married couple agreed that "the valleys are mighty gloomy at times, but we have something great going for us—we're *together* in them!"

Even brief, minor illnesses can upset the normal pattern of mutual need satisfaction by which the hungers of the heart are fed and marriages are kept going and growing. Bob Essex becomes withdrawn whenever his wife Sally suffers from even a cold. His "nobody home" periods (as she calls them) produce feelings of rejection in her which are expressed in angry verbal attacks. Bob's withdrawal illustrates the way leftover feelings from childhood can influence marriages. In his boyhood, his mother had used her sicknesses to manipulate her family. Now, his slumbering boy-feelings of resentment of this are awakened by his wife's minor illnesses. He is "parentifying" his spouse and responding as if she were about to manipulate him by her sniffles (which actually does not happen). This response and resulting conflict block their ability to satisfy each other's personal and sexual needs. Fortunately, Bob and Sally were able to discuss their problem frankly—after the storm. Each leveled with the other about the painful feelings which started their cycle of mutual starvation. As a result, they gradually became able to interrupt their cycles sooner, and even to keep some from starting. It was in a marital growth group, led by a group counselor and sponsored by their church, that Bob came to understand the origins of his "ghost feelings" from the past.

Illnesses of children arouse deep anxieties in parents, frequently accompanied by resentments and guilt. One mother reports, "Whenever Joan catches even a slight cold, I imagine the worst and become terribly overprotective." Parents often experience a child as a part of their own identity (which, incidentally, complicates the child's search for his autonomous identity). A child's pain is felt vicariously by the parents. Furthermore, a child's sickness or injury creates a threat to the dreams and hopes which his parents have invested in him. Some of the ways the child has fed parental needs—e.g., through responding satisfyingly and by being happy, healthy, and successful—are interrupted. Serious illness or handicaps threaten or cut off other satisfactions which children bring parents—e.g., physical immortality, reassurances of masculinity or femininity, promise of support as adults of aging parents. Most parents relive their own childhood and youth through their growing children; their sicknesses may arouse old fears of being hurt or of dying, from their early lives. The heavy physical and emotional drain on the parents (particularly the mother of a sick child) causes fatigue and gobbles up the hours, leaving little time or energy for re-creating companionship or sex play. Growing hunger of the parents often emerges as anger, turned toward the child in resentment, toward the self in depression, or toward the partner in conflict.

The illness of a spouse or child frequently arouses conflicted feelings about the *giving* and *receiving* balance in the relationship. In the give and take of family life, a sick child or adult cannot give as he could in health. Instead, he "takes" much more than before in care, worry and attention. Furthermore, he may be irritable and demanding, particularly if he is in pain or has been pampered previously. Because of the male cult of self-sufficiency, many men feel unmasculine when sickness forces them to be dependent on others.

GUIDELINES FOR THE FAMILY CRISIS OF ILLNESS

The principles of crisis counseling are now reasonably clear, thanks to several decades of experience and research by the mental health professions. These can be applied by many couples to their marital and family crises. Here are some guidelines based on the principles:

1) *Turn toward other people for support and help:* Many families worsen their health crises by turning away from others or they are socially isolated and have no "significant others" available. People need people; especially when the going is rough. Then it is crucial to avoid the go-it-alone trap by finding help (e.g., a clergyman, neighbor, social agency worker, or the helpful type of relative) in sharing the load. Illness is usually bad enough; lonely illness is much worse! The inner circle of the family needs support from the "extended family"—the next circle out from the center. This is a natural ministry for the lay members of a church or synagogue—to be a part of the extended family of those in crises. While the six-year-old son of one couple was hospitalized in a coma, friends from their church's young marrieds group gave massive caring and support, bringing dishes of food and baby-sitting while the parents spent anguished hours at the hospital. This group was practicing the biblical injunction, "Bear one another's burdens." Whatever the health crisis, the rule of thumb is *get and stay connected with people who care!*

2) *Talk out burdensome feelings surrounding the problem:* Bottling up big feelings such as fear, frustration, guilt, anger, loneliness, resentment, confusion, helplessness, failure or hopelessness is like storing dynamite in the basement. Draining them off, through talking them through with someone in confidence, prevents them from becoming explosive and frees the person to think more clearly and act more constructively. The key to handling family stress creatively is to keep the husband-wife and parent-child communication lines open. Identifying inappropriate ghost feelings (e.g., Bob Essex's), and discussing them fully, usually robs them of their power to foul up relationships, even if the origins of the feelings are not discovered. The crucial feelings are those around the particular problem and near the surface, but previously not faced and discussed. Digging for remote feelings

is unnecessary in most crisis counseling. You don't need to know how a fire started to put it out. It is unnecessary to be a prisoner of the past if one is willing to face lingering ghost feelings and make a determined effort to improve one's present relationships.

If repeated attempts to communicate on significant levels fail, it is a sign of strength to do as the Knudsens did—seek the help of a well-trained counselor. Couples with relatively healthy marriages which have been thrown off balance by a crisis usually are able to use short-term marriage counseling in decisively constructive ways.

Increasing numbers of congregations are training lay "pastoral care teams" to provide a ministry of listening and befriending for persons in crisis. Such teams should be trained to provide this help for families who are caught in crises of illness and disability.

3) *Review the situation objectively, boiling the problem down to its essentials:* Discussing a complex problem with an understanding person helps one accomplish these goals—gain an awareness of the way the difficulty started and how it grew; separate the parts of the problem and get some perspective on their relative importance; identify those things which can be changed; explore alternative ways of handling these, including probable consequences. "I felt so engulfed by our mass of problems, I couldn't think clearly about any of them," declared a young husband whose wife was hospitalized. Discussing their crisis at length with a favorite uncle allowed him to gain objectivity and to plan his strategy for taking action to lighten the load and to acquire additional help in bearing it.

4) *Begin to do something constructive, however small:* This is known as "action therapy." The personality is something like a muscle. When it is partially paralyzed (by indecision, pressure, fear or guilt), it grows weaker. When one feels trapped in a family crisis, it is essential to challenge oneself to take that first small step. This helps to break the vicious cycles of fear, anger, guilt, and withdrawal which cause marital fights and family crises

to escalate. One couple with a long-sick child began to break out of their "squirrel cage" (vicious cycle) of emotional exhaustion, frustration, and total emotional investment in the child when they took themselves in hand and brought Grandmother to stay with the child for a long evening. Dinner out and time alone together revived their spirits. (Senior citizens groups in churches can help by providing "substitute grandmothers" for young couples whose parents are far away. This can be mutually enriching.)

Recognizing that in any situation something *can* be done (even if only changing one's attitude toward it) and *doing it* has several benefits, in addition to interrupting the snowballing of problems. It awakens hope, reduces depression, and begins the rebuilding of self-confidence. These feelings, in turn, release energies to take further constructive steps. The first steps are often hard ones, but there is no other way to move.

5) *Learn how to find and draw on spiritual resources:* The crises of illness and disability can serve the useful function of exposing the need for a viable philosophy of life (that makes sense to the individual) and for a growing, trustful relationship with God. During her recovery from a cancer operation, a young mother told her priest, "This brush with death has forced me to look at my life in a new way. Many things that seemed important, look trivial now. I've decided to stop running and start living—to try to be more alive to my kids and my husband and my friends, to enjoy each day and to work at deepening my spiritual life." Illness and accidents crack the fragile shell of our self-sufficiency; they expose our inner emptiness, our "value vacuum" (Viktor Frankl); they increase the volume of the background music—the knowledge that we must someday die—which plays faintly in the distance at other times. A West Coast physician asks his patients who have recovered from heart attacks, "What have you learned from this experience?" What many people learn from such experiences is to value life as never before, to come alive to other people and to the Divine Spirit, to reinvest their precious days

and years in causes that matter, and thus to become a part of that stream of humanity that will go on long after they are gone.

Persons who are spiritually impoverished when crises strike should ask for the help of a priest, minister, or rabbi. He is trained in the skills of removing blocks to spiritual growth and in making the riches of a religious heritage available to individuals in need. It is always wise to inform one's clergyman of any serious medical problem. He can bring spiritual resources to bear on that vertical dimension of problems where medical and psychological resources are not relevant or helpful. In some cases he can awaken an awareness of the Divine Presence; equally important, he may help to release those healing forces within the person which have been blocked by guilt, anger, fear or hate.

COPING WITH CHRONIC ILLNESSES AND HANDICAPS

The painful effects of many illnesses and accidents are bearable in part because the persons involved are aware that "this, too, shall pass." But each year hundreds of thousands of families face health problems the effects of which do *not* pass. After the acute phase of the crisis is over, they must learn to live with some chronic disability, often of major proportions.

"Your child will be handicapped to some degree." The neurologist's words cut like a cold steel knife; as Jack and Patricia Doyle listen, their worst fears are confirmed. Their dreams for their little girl are crushed in an instant "that seemed like a nightmare." The birth of a handicapped child can tear your marriage apart or it can weld it more tightly, depending on your emotional maturity and joint skill in coping with your negative feelings and the objective problems.

Shift from the obstetrical ward to the post-surgical recovery unit of the same hospital. Jim Andersen was brought to the emergency room four hours ago, after a head-on collision on his way to work. The surgeon tells Jim's wife, Beatrice: "Your husband is past the critical period but he will have to be hospitalized for at least four months. There may be some permanent disability in the use of his legs." The Doyles and the Andersens are facing crises which probably will change their lives in deep and permanent ways. Such crises often hit when least expected. They come in many forms —surgery or accidents which cripple; fast-moving or protracted fatal illnesses; chronic debilitating conditions; loss of sight, hearing or speech; health problems of aging spouses or parents; mental and emotional illnesses. These crises come as rude intruders, disrupting the mutual need-satisfaction patterns of family life in countless ways.

The five guidelines offered above for coping with short-term, less serious illnesses also apply to chronic and handicapping conditions. In fact, it is even more crucial to use them in handling the family problems related to the latter. Building on the previous guidelines, here are some additional pointers for coping with the continuing burdens of chronic problems.

6) *Face all the facts, both painful and hopeful:* A psychologist who knows the struggles of the handicapped from personal experience declares, "It will help you a great deal if you begin by learning all the facts about your child's handicap. . . . You should know how handicapped he is likely to be and for how long." Some parents respond to a suspected handicap with the psychological defense of denial. This may cause them to delay obtaining a medical evaluation, reject the diagnosis when they do get it, or go "doctor shopping," searching for someone who will tell them their child is normal or can recover. Others pursue faith healers while delaying obtaining medical help. In contrast, the Doyles had a long talk with their doctor who described therapies for cerebral palsy, its causes, and the prognosis for their child. This knowledge reduced their irrational fears and helped them plan for the future.

7) *Obtain the best help available without delay:* Encouraging new therapies for helping the handicapped achieve lives of maximum usefulness and satisfaction are becoming increasingly avail-

able. Included are physical therapies, retraining techniques, speech therapy and, in some cases, restorative or corrective surgery. Reaching out for help lets the handicapped person and the family discover that they are not alone. They find that many others have like problems and that there are organized groups which are concerned about each major handicap. Working with these volunteer groups gives them the continuing friendship of those with a common concern and an opportunity to do something constructive to further research and therapy. Reaching for help also brings awareness of the network of centers and services dedicated to helping persons with problems like theirs. One directory of services for the handicapped lists over 330 centers in the United States. Some churches and synagogues provide religious education for the homebound handicapped and sharing groups for parents of handicapped children.

8) *Work to develop freeing attitudes*: A consultant of the National Society for Crippled Children and Adults observes, "The psychological effects of handicaps are frequently more crippling than the physical disability. . . . Attitudes of the individual, the family, and the community toward the handicapped person are basic to the emotional color in each individual case." Religious groups, as attitude molders, have a role in helping to build enlightened, accepting attitudes toward the permanently disabled. Parents contribute most to the development of the child's realistic self-acceptance by loving and accepting him *as he is*—with a handicap. Parents do well to remind themselves that "the cultivation of a constructive relationship between parent and child is as important as any effort to improve the physical condition of the child."

Negative, conflicting feelings—the handicapped person's and his family's—should be talked through, perhaps with an understanding friend, clergyman or counselor. A study of 64 parents of disabled children revealed that the great majority had strong feelings of resentment and irritability toward their children, mixed with love for them. A report on the family crisis revolving around a retarded child concludes: "Parental guilt is universal." A handicapped person *is* a burden at times! Occasional resentment and anger is therefore normal. Only when such feelings are denied and ignored do they accumulate until they block constructive relationships.

Persons handicapped in adulthood have more difficult psychological adjustments than the handicapped-from-birth who have never known normal living. A major physical disability may shatter the person's self-image and his confidence. The process of grief which follows any major loss is long and painful. The uphill struggles in learning to walk, talk, or feed oneself take guts on the person's part and encouragement from those who love and respect him. Psychiatrist Karl Menninger describes what is required: "The permanently disabled person must accept his handicap—not surrender to it." In rebuilding his fragmented self-image, the person needs to see that (as one man put it), he "is not a short leg with a man attached, but a *man* with a short leg."

The growth of freeing attitudes (by the person and his family) is sometimes blocked by distorted theology which attributes diseases and handicaps to God's punishment. (Such a punitive picture of deity is less than flattering to God.) The Jewish, Catholic, and Protestant views all reject this conception of handicaps. They see God as a loving father who wills wholeness and health for all his children. The fulfillment of his will often is stymied by the incompleteness of the creative evolutionary process (which incompleteness challenges man to conquer cancer and other diseases, and thus to help complete creation). God's will is also blocked by the misuse of man's freedom in living that violates, often unknowingly, the principles of health. It is undeniable that there are many tragedies which no philosophy or religious view renders comprehensible; but it only makes the problem worse to attribute it to God's punishment. The common response, "What have I done to deserve *this*?" assumes that persons hit by suffering must have done something to deserve it (a view attacked by the Book of Job), or that God has somehow "done one dirt." The basic assumption is what is in error here. Living a religious life is *not* a guarantee that one will avoid suffering; it *is* a source of tremendous help in handling suffering creatively. The feeling that one's handicap is an evidence that one has been discriminated against is sometimes dispelled by the discovery that suffering is a part of the fabric from which everyone's life is cut and that nearly everyone has some thorn in the flesh. The size of or absence of a handicap is no indicator of the measure of one's sins. The approach of sound religion is to avoid any form of judgmentalism and to exercise acceptance and compassion toward all who suffer.

9) *Encourage the person to achieve his maximum independence and social usefulness:* It is "cruel kindness" to do anything for a handicapped person that he can learn to do for himself. The heartache or guilt of parents may cause them to "help" their spastic child in ways that prevent him from acquiring through struggle the skills on which his independence and self-confidence must be based. Some parents report feelings of chronic grief ("living under a dark cloud") and personal inadequacy because of a handicapped child. These feelings may cause them to push the child toward unrealistic goals, thus consigning him to a *failure cycle* (each failure makes the next failure more certain).

Whatever is done to assist the handicapped should be done in light of what will contribute to the mental health of the whole family. Institutionalizing a severely disabled child often is necessary for the well-being of other family members, as well as to provide proper therapies.

The goal for a handicapped person is to help him equip or re-equip himself to live life as fully and productively as he is able, within his limitations, developing as many of his God-given potentialities and contributing as much to society as possible. One of his assets which should be fostered is that of *constructive overcompensation*—the human genius of offsetting lost or missing functions by excelling in the use of those one possesses. Helen Keller was one of many remarkable examples of this ability to "turn handicaps into handles." Furthermore, the sufferings and victories of handicapped persons can equip them to be of special help to others. Such persons have an entree to the inner worlds of other sufferers. The recovered alcoholics in A.A., who have demonstrated this principle thousands of times, have a well-known prayer that summarizes the life task of any handicapped person and his family: "Grant me the serenity to accept the things I cannot change; the courage to change the things I can; and the wisdom to know the difference." One New York psychiatrist states that if a patient after three years of psychotherapy has really learned to live by these principles, the therapy has been a success. The philosophy of this A.A. prayer can help to guide a married couple through the many periods of shadow and sunlight in their life together.

20

Mixed Marriages—Making Them Work!

•

FREDERICK W. BRINK

Frederick W. Brink, a Captain in the Chaplain Corps of the United States Navy, is presently stationed at the Naval Training Center, Orlando, Florida. He was formerly on the staff of the Chief of Chaplains in Washington, D.C. Because of his deep pastoral interest in the men with whom he works, he has written several booklets and articles on questions related to marriage and family life.

•

JUDAISM, ROMAN CATHOLICISM, PROTESTANTISM, WOULD ALL AGREE that marriage is a relationship instituted by God for the welfare and the happiness of mankind. The relationship is of man, but it is perfected by the blessing of God. In it a man and woman tie themselves together in a manner acceptable to God, for their mutual growth, benefit and happiness. Legal authority of the state is recognized as essential for the continuation of an orderly and moral society. But the paramount authority belongs to God, with the marriage existing in its final essence and worth only when it has God's approval.

The marriage is before God more than before men. The parties enter it with the deliberate intention of including God in every relationship that the marriage may one day embrace. Only marriages where this intent is present, and which are as God's laws permit, can expect God's blessing.

Such a marriage is very much the individual's own before God, subject to God's approval more than the approval of any one church body or clergyman. The rabbi, the priest, the minister, are witnesses, not the originators, of the marriage being established before God. They are the spokesmen to point out that marriage is more a process than an event. Marriage does not come full-blown as a result of the words of an officiating clergyman. Marriage continues as a process of growth in which all of life's varied experiences are shared as gifts and responsibilities from God Himself.

While all three of the great faiths would agree that some such statement as this describes in general terms the essence of marriage and the relationship of the contracting parties to God and to God's laws, additional considerations of special concern to their adherents would be added by both the Roman Catholic and the Jewish faiths. Within these added considerations lie some of the major problems that confront interfaith marriages.

The traditional Roman Catholic interpretation tends to consider the approval of God and the participation of the Roman Catholic Church as synonymous. Since the Roman Catholic believes that his is the one true Church, then for him the Church speaks authoritatively for God. And since the Church speaks for God it has the right to limit, for its own adherents, the conditions under which the marriage can be consummated. These conditions include: marriage ceremony before a priest of the Roman Catholic Church; the obligation that all children born to the marriage be baptized and reared in the Roman Catholic Church; the obligation of the Roman Catholic party to follow the rules of the Church in faith and practice. These rules, in turn, include not only required attendance at the services of the Church, but a restriction on active participation in other forms of worship than those of the Roman Catholic Church, and the planning for parenthood only within the manner allowed by the Church.

The Jew who marries a non-Jew, while echoing the importance of having the marriage meet the approval of God, brings to the marriage two other very important considerations: the unique place of the family in Judaism, and the national heritage and identity of the Jewish people. A non-Jew, marrying a religious Jew, will find himself or herself caught up in the family and the heritage of the Jewish partner in a much more realistic fashion and to a much deeper degree than would a partner to some other type of religiously mixed marriage. Place will have to constantly be made in the non-Jew's thinking for the preservation of the Jewish peoplehood and culture and for a total relationship with the Jewish family. As one Jewish Navy chaplain has written: "One has not gotten to the heart of Judaism and the concept of Jewish peoplehood unless he grasps the great ethical principle of the sanctity of the home. . . . More even than the synagogue, the Jew and his faith have survived the long trek of history because of the moral, ethical, and religious teachings the family absorbed in the Jewish home."

A word should be added in this general consideration about another type of interdenominational marriage—the marriage of two Protestants or two Jews from radically different denominational backgrounds. Normally, the marriage of two Protestants or Jews faces only the decision as to which denomination they will jointly embrace. But despite all the moves and impetus toward church union and ecumenicity, there still exist Protestant and Jewish denominations that claim unique authority and believe they possess the only acceptable form of worship and expression. A marriage that ties together a sincere adherent of one of these denominations with a partner from a more liberal group could result in contention as bitter as any between Protestant and Catholic, or Christian and Hebrew. The partner reared in a highly liturgical denomination may be mismated with one reared in a tradition that rejects most or all liturgical forms. The partner whose conviction causes him to look on every person outside his particular denomination as "unsaved" may be mismated with one holding a more tolerant view.

There is a biblical phrase that warns against hitching a horse and an ox to the same plow. They pull with different motions and with different strength. They are really not suited to work as a team. Just so, all of the three great religious groups join in the same view regarding mixed marriage: warning that the linking of Protestant with Roman Catholic, Christian with Jew, or for that matter a religiously minded person with a nonreligious person, invites difficulties in the marriage. All of the faiths simply say: if this is your intention, consider, then reconsider, and then if at all possible, decide against such a tie.

Most of the literature regarding mixed marriages is addressed to persons still anticipating marriage. The tendency therefore is to think mainly in terms of overcoming barriers to such a union, rather than recognizing that there will be continuing problems. When the barriers have been overcome and the marriage has taken place, the interfaith situation remains. If the marriage is to be successful, that situation must be faced not once but a multitude of times, and not by fiat but by continuing adjustment and understanding.

THREATS TO THE SECURITY OF THE MARRIAGE

The mixture of religious faiths poses threats to the security of a marriage in the very areas that should be points of strength and harmony. Some of these threats are enumerated here, not so much to discourage such marriages as to aid those already so married in mastering the difficulties.

1) *In the area of worship.* The experience of worshipping God and of being conscious of his presence in the home is both an individual and a corporate experience. Trying to follow two separate courses of religious experience within the marriage can only tend to emphasize the individual experience and make

difficult the corporate one. Common worship and common involvement in the practice of religion and the expression of faith is one of the strongest ties between a husband and wife. It forms a deeply significant resource for marital health and happiness. A continuing difference of religious faith and expression tends to erase this resource and imperil this tie.

2) *In the area of children.* Where present, children form an integral part of a successful marriage. It took both parents in harmony to bring the children into the family. Both parents should remain equally involved in every aspect of their children's lives and training. A maintained difference in religious faiths not only robs the parents of their common relationship in the training and guidance of the children; it prevents one or the other from bringing to the children the best spiritual heritage he or she knows.

There is an effect also on the child. The maintained difference in the religious faith of the parents tends to divide loyalties, encouraging the child to depend on one parent more than the other, or to be suspicious of one parent, when the dependence and the confidence should be toward both parents equally.

3) *In the area of companionship between the husband and wife.* The goal of any significant marriage, and certainly of any religiously oriented marriage, is the sharing of all the elements and experiences of life by husband with wife, wife with husband. To be required to fence off whole areas of experience and activity by following separate religious paths cannot help but make difficult, if not actually destroy, the motivations and support that spring from a commonly held and expressed reservoir of faith.

4) *In the area of the intimacies of marriage and the accompanying area of family planning.* The wisdom of God, which made man and woman sexually different and yet sexually dependent on each other, gave to the marriage relationship a sharing quality without equal. Out of that relationship springs, on occasion, new life. When a difference in religious faith fosters a difference of conscience in the matter of planning parenthood, the intimacies

of marital love might well be changed from an arena of affection into a battleground of enmity.

5) *In the area of wider family relationships.* In a Christian-Jewish marriage, the feeling of being an outsider to the heritage of the family can be very real and destructive. In any mixed-religion marriage, parents of the couple may show more prejudice than the parties themselves and wreak havoc in the harmony of the home as a result. While it is true that a husband and wife marry each other rather than each other's families, they cannot ignore the attitudes and the influence the respective family ties will have on their marriage.

Simply stated, the truth is that religious faith and practice cannot be isolated from the other experiences of marriage. A person's set of values, the motivation for his attitudes and actions, his whole reason and purpose in life, are linked to what he believes and how he expresses that belief. Consciously or unconsciously, every significant relationship of a marriage is colored and influenced by the religious convictions of the partners. Similar convictions engender harmony and strength. Dissimilar convictions engender disharmony and weakness.

SOLUTIONS TO THE RELIGIOUS DIFFERENCES

The possible difficulties that face mixed marriage can be enumerated and expanded far beyond what has been said. But the important consideration is what can be done by two persons joined in an interfaith marriage to solve the difficulties. Three possible solutions are suggested here.

One solution would be to preserve the different traditions of the partners. Husband and wife would each go his/her own religious way, containing separate observances, in large degree independently of each other.

This solution would demand that each partner maintain a

deliberate and continuing attempt to understand and respect the other's faith and its requirements, to discuss without rancor or accusation what the faiths stand for and demand, to substitute knowledge for emotion, and to recognize and respect the sincerity of each other's tradition. It would demand that each partner not only permit but encourage and assist the other in the observance of his individual religious duties and practices. (For example: cheerful participation as baby-sitter so the other could observe occasions of worship, or chauffeuring the other or the children to religious observances in which the chauffeur would not be joining.) It would certainly demand the support by one of the partners in the religious education of the children along lines that might be alien to the one giving the support. Above all it would demand that each partner be true to his own religious faith and be active in that faith, even while respecting the faith of the other, and expect the other partner to do the same.

The danger in this solution is readily apparent. In the interests of avoiding argument or disagreement, one or both of the partners may suffer a weakening of religious allegiance or its abandonment (perhaps only by neglect) and thus lose the benefit of the heritage of faith. Or it may result in serious friction within the family when the inconveniences that are necessary to permit the partners to go their separate ways become points of contention. Religion should be a tie between the partners to a marriage, not an occasion for separation.

Another possible solution would be to have the partners compromise on a middle ground and embrace a mutually acceptable religious allegiance. Such a solution would involve a serious study by both partners of their respective religious heritages, then of other traditions and heritages, and finally a settling on one which comes somewhere between the original two. A mutual compromise would be the result. In effect, each partner would set aside the elements of birth and childhood training, would rethink all of religion in terms of what he or she actually believes, and start afresh, regardless of what their formative years had contributed.

The difficulty, of course, is that few persons are emotionally or mentally equipped to make such a study and transition. One does not easily rid himself/herself of heritage, of beliefs instilled in childhood, of all the influences which originally inculcated these religious beliefs. The danger is that, instead of settling on a common allegiance, they will settle for nothing, ending with a religious vacuum rather than a religious reservoir.

Parenthetically, it must be said that this cannot be the solution for a sincerely devout believer who has been taught that the only avenue of salvation is in his denomination and who accepts the strictures of that group as the equivalent of the strictures of God Himself. For such a partner in the marriage, there can be no compromise.

A *third solution would* take into consideration the relative depth and significance of the religious faiths of the two partners, and *have the one with the lesser depth of faith give up his or her inherited faith and fully embrace the faith and practice of the other.* In essence this would mean that each party would ask: "Can I find as much meaning and spiritual support in my partner's faith as I have found in my own? If I tried, could I come to God as readily if I were a Catholic instead of a Protestant, if I were a Protestant instead of a Catholic, if I were a Christian instead of a Jew, if I were a Jew instead of a Christian?" Then, if the answers were in the affirmative, sincerely and with appropriate study for understanding, a change to the faith of the partner would take place.

Such a solution could not be in word alone. It would have to be complete, and it would have to be sincere. Anything less would become, at some future time, a ground for contention when a friction based on some other element in the marriage arose and the one who had changed faiths used the change as a ground for recrimination and blame.

THE ULTIMATE REQUIREMENT
FOR A SUCCESSFUL MIXED MARRIAGE

Whatever the solution to the differences in religious heritage, one basic requirement exists if a mixed marriage is to succeed. The home must be made a center of constructive religious living and thinking. It should foster at all times a dependence on God's wisdom and support and a sense of partnership with God that is real and vital. It must include regular, deliberate observances of individual and corporate worship in which the children and both parents are involved. Under no circumstances should a difference in the religious faiths of the parents be allowed to create a religious vacuum in the home or result in a family where that difference erases or obstructs the influence of God upon all within it.

If the different faiths are to be maintained, the children as they mature should be instructed in the history and tradition of each faith, even though they are officially identified with one. They should be helped to understand that God can be approached along different paths by different people, and yet remain the same God. They should be shown that the approach to God is more important than the name of the pathway that leads to Him, or the structures that line the pathway. They should be trained in their formative years by precept and by the example of both parents, learning not that one parent is right and the other is wrong, but that both parents have a meaningful relationship with the same God, and they too must have such a relationship.

The religious training of the children must never be allowed to become a battleground for conflict or division between the parents. Nor should the religious training of the children be omitted in the mistaken attitude of avoiding confusion in the children's minds or of "waiting until they are old enough to decide for themselves." The most tragic situation in a mixed marriage occurs when the purely sectarian aspects of religious belief become stronger than the love the parents have for each other and for their children.

In our psychology-minded American society it is important to recognize that religious differences are often made the battleground on which differences of an entirely alien origin are fought out. In anger or in pique, one partner turns on the other's religious faith to voice a tension that rises from a totally unrelated source. Parents must be ever on the alert to keep their religious beliefs, even though varying, as sources of strength and security and not let them become covers for disagreements in personality.

In honesty it must be admitted that because of the strict rules placed on Roman Catholics, and because of the emotional overtones of strong group loyalty in a Jewish-Christian marriage, it is in one case the Protestant and in the other case the non-Jew who will probably have to make the most concessions toward religious harmony. Their reactions will usually determine the success or failure of the union in so far as that success or failure is influenced by religion. But even if called upon to make concessions, that partner still retains a positive responsibility for the success of the marriage and for the religious education of the children. Ethically, a man may give up some of what he considers his rights in the cause of harmony (as long as he does not violate his conscience in so doing), but he cannot give up his responsibility for that harmony.

The summation of the whole problem is simple. Over the years marriages between persons of differing religious faiths have proven subject to peculiar stresses and strains. Persons holding similar faiths have largely been spared these particular strains. Since any marriage, even the best, is subject to periodic difficulties and a difference in religious faiths seems to add an extra difficulty, all of the religious traditions unite in trying to discourage the establishment of interfaith marriages.

But once established, all of the religious traditions agree that success in the marriage will come in direct proportion to each partner's sincerity in attempting to understand the other's faith and its claims upon him, in direct proportion to each partner's sincerity in encouraging the other to maintain an active personal faith, and in direct proportion to each partner's full participation in the religious activities of the home, jointly, singly, and with the children.

When together the partners to the marriage place their hands in the hand of God and seek his help in meeting every problem as it arises, the labels of their faith become unimportant.

21

Marriages in Difficulty

•

JESHAIA SCHNITZER

Jeshaia Schnitzer, Rabbi of Temple Shomrei Emunah, Montclair, N.J., is an author appearing widely in professional periodicals and lecturer on marriage topics, a member of the American Association of Marriage Counselors, the Montclair Child Guidance Clinic, the Tri-State Family Relations Council, the National Association of Social Workers, and many other organizations; he is also actively engaged in important communal services.

•

IN EVERY GENERATION MEN AND WOMEN HAVE JOINED HANDS in matrimony to fulfill their most essential needs of love, sex, children, and other deep human longings.

In every period of history and each generation, the needs of marriage have differed, even as its stresses and strains have varied. It is a tribute to the resourcefulness of the human being that throughout the ages husbands and wives adapted themselves to the marital requirements of their times. In this way they were able to find fulfillment of their many needs, and in turn they strengthened the institution of marriage and the family. Strong family life helped give stability and continuity to the fabric of human society.

We have seen tremendous changes in the twentieth century, created by science and technological advancements; we have also seen how drastically they affect the stability of marriage and family life. Marriage in the second half of the twentieth century has a new face, and people are demanding more from it for their personal fulfillment than ever before. With these rapid changes and new expectations have come many challenges. Often couples have either not been able to meet the challenges or have been frustrated by setting too many high and unreachable goals for their marriages. The result has been a gradual rise in the breakdown of marriages and an increasing number of divorces. This holds particularly true for America, as shown by the high statistics on divorce since World War II.

In a chapter on the "Socio-Demographic Aspects of Divorce," William M. Kephart of the University of Pennsylvania writes the following on the United States' divorce rate:

> During the colonial period, divorce was a rare phenomenon; as a matter of fact, up to the time of the Civil War, divorce was not considered numerically important enough to warrant the collection of national figures. In the mid-1800's, as a concomitant of the woman's rights movement, divorce laws were liberalized, and by the 1860's various anti-feminist groups, fearful that family values were being undermined, demanded that national divorce figures be tabulated. The initial tabulations, published by the Census Bureau, were for the year 1867. The total number of divorces in that year was 9,927. Eighty years later, in 1946—the record year—the number had risen to 616,000.

This sociologist points out that considering the population growth and utilizing the figures of the 1960 census, divorces in the United States have increased about eight times as fast as the population. In the postwar period, 1946–1960, more than 6,000,000 divorces were granted. He estimates that by 1970 census the postwar figure will easily have exceeded 10,000,000 divorces. The general impression among sociologists and family life educators is that about one out of every four marriages in the United States ends in divorce.

What has brought about such chaos and disorder in marriage today? This is not the place to consider all of the social, economic, and ideological changes in the twentieth century which have had their direct influence on marriage and the family. Nevertheless, we ought to consider and try to understand the processes and the attitudes which create distrust, anger, alienation in marriage as well as the other circumstances leading to the final disintegration. Perhaps the quickest way, for our purpose here, is to ask what it is that men and women expect of marriage today.

What are the demands and the expectations that people place upon marriage today? What does it take to make a marriage partnership effective and sustaining? What are the ingredients that create wholesome and vibrant marriages, fulfilling the deep needs and the high expectations of men and women today?

In discussing these very questions, Dr. Leon J. Saul, in his book *Fidelity and Infidelity, and What Makes or Breaks a Marriage,* maintains that in order to have "reasonable harmony in marriage" each partner must contribute a number of components. In capsule form, the following are the required ingredients for a harmonious marriage according to this psychiatrist:

1) Love—a desire to be with and close to a partner, without ulterior or egocentric motives.
2) Sexual attractiveness—the desire and healthy functioning and enjoyment of sex.
3) A sense of romance—the end result of many elements, adding up to what we call "being in love."
4) Parenthood—one of the deepest and most enduring satisfactions that life affords.
5) Responsibility—includes the children's direct emotional need of parents; the breadwinning responsibility of the husband and the wife's responsibility for everything which makes a home.
6) Maturity—each partner relatively independent, giving and

able with minimal hostility and competitiveness to live and
let live.

7) Fit and mesh—the more adequate one fulfills the six components listed above and the more adequate the outgrowing
of childhood patterns in favor of mature attitudes and feelings, the easier, freer and more harmonious are the relationships in the family.

Clergymen who have engaged in premarital interviews with
young couples will testify that most couples believe they can bring
to their marriages these components. The young people believe
they have these components and contributions to share, because,
as they say, they "are in love and love is the most important thing
in life." They have been carried away by the influences of our age,
which emphasize the romanticism of love, the deep need for sexual expression; and they see their compatibility (the fit and mesh)
in the many leisure pursuits they have followed in the period of
their engagement. They generally apply to themselves the more
commonly used term of "compatibility." They speak about the
way they can respond to the other's needs and how well they
seem to feel and understand the reactions and needs of their
loved one.

Many couples speak glibly about responsibility, but they do
not comprehend the total meaning of responsibility in marriage.
They cannot visualize the demands that marriage places upon
people as mates, as parents, as breadwinner and homemaker, and
later in life as in-laws. Many young people do not know what it
means to love. They have not been given the love and direction
by their parents to enable them to grow and mature and in turn
to love others and serve as model parents.

Learning how to love is fundamental to making a good marriage.
When we learn how to love, we also gain the ability to give more
than we receive. Marriage is never a fifty-fifty proposition. Sometimes one partner has to give more—as much as 60 or 70 percent—

and at other times the other one has to be able to pitch in the extra share. This is not easy to learn or to achieve, especially for Americans. Rugged individualism, which is still part of our way of life, and the competitiveness which is encouraged throughout the formative years of childhood in school and sports and later in college and the business world, does not make for the kind of people who can easily give and take, or fit and mesh. Can we expect a man and a woman who have been exposed to the game of competitiveness all their lives suddenly to be transformed when they say the words "I do"? By falling in love and experiencing a wedding ceremony can they become people who do not need to compete but who can share and at times even give more than one's share?

In quick succession we have enumerated those components which make for difficulty in marriage: a lack of responsibility, a lack of love to help one to grow and mature, the inability to give more than one receives, and the projection of one's competitiveness in the marriage arrangement. Brief case histories dealing with each of the above situations could be helpful to a fuller understanding of the dynamics which set in motion the processes of anger, disillusionment, distrust, alienation, and finally the disintegration of the relationship.

RESPONSIBILITY

The responsibility of breadwinner is most important for the man, but no less significant is the role of homemaking for the woman. Poor functioning or indifference to homemaking on the part of the wife can easily undermine the confidence and trust of a man in his mate and the marriage.

Molly and Bill are two highly intelligent people and before their marriage both held responsible positions and were socially very active. After marriage Bill went into business and now operates an aluminum product construction company, working long and tedious hours, both at his office and on job sites. He is a fairly good provider, though much of his income is being reinvested into the company. Bill makes no great demands upon his wife. Molly, who was a competent secretary before her marriage, has not worked since marrying Bill. Molly is not too appreciative of Bill's sacrifices and his hard work, nor is she careful in her purchases and the way she spends money, either for herself or the household. Molly basically despises doing housework, makes no apology about it, and never completes her chores. The house is seldom clean and neat, and the refrigerator is usually empty and messy. Dinner is never on time, and then it is served grudgingly. Molly is always ready to be taken out for dinner or a social engagement, but she will never offer to invite Bill's business associates to the house for an evening. She further eludes her duties by imposing some chores upon Bill when he is at home or has an afternoon off from work.

Unless Molly can be helped by her counselor to break away from the housekeeping patterns of her mother, who had a husband who was a traveling salesman and was seldom at home, this marriage will be endangered. Bill comes from a home where his mother was meticulous in her housekeeping and showed constant concern for the needs of her husband and children. For Bill, marriage is a well-kept home and a wife who cares for the things that matter to a man. This case, like so many that are seen in the office of a marriage counselor, is a childish rejection of domestic responsibility, and one will have to help these wives to understand the roots of their behavior and make the necessary adjustments.

INABILITY TO LOVE AND SHARE MUTUALLY

Harry, who came from a lower-middle-class home, has felt that the war and his father both did him a great injustice. He started college before the war but was drafted, and after the war his father pushed him to find work, and so he never completed his education. Harry is highly intelligent, very verbal, and could have done well in any field had he completed his college studies. He has never tried to do his best in his sales work and never provided adequately for his wife and three children. But somehow he manages to keep some of the bills paid and his wife always worrying how they will manage financially the following week. Evelyn, his wife, is meticulous and exacting in her housework. She is not demanding in any way, either for herself or the children, and shows concern for Harry and his bewilderment. Evelyn has never been a very outgoing person or lavish in her emotional feelings toward Harry. In the course of the years the strains of managing a household on a shoestring and the frustrations of not earning an adequate livelihood have taken their toll on the emotional life of this couple. Communications and mutual understanding have so deteriorated that for more than ten years Harry and Evelyn have had no sexual relations. Seldom is there now a kind word or an embrace. Harry, resentful of his father and frustrated by his own lack of stamina and willpower to further his career, continually stints in his efforts at work. Lacking the love and warmth which he desperately needs and no longer receives from either his wife or his children, he tends to drift. He makes little effort and for years has remained stunted in his growth toward a mature attitude to work or to his marriage. How much longer can such a marriage go on? Where can the powers and strengths be found to overcome the increasing number of difficulties in this family?

FIT AND MESH IN MARRIAGE

Jack and Nancy are a couple who have had many turbulent years of marriage. They have three lovely children, a beautiful home, and many friends. Jack is in a thriving real estate business which has brought him great financial success and even some recognition in the field of banking and finance. Nancy, though a bit withdrawn and reticent, is a warm person and a loving mother to her children. She admires her husband for his accomplishments and says that she is ready to fulfill his wishes. She manages her large household fairly competently and works hard to keep up with the demands of a busy social life, schoolchildren, and a large, spacious home. Yet Jack is never satisfied with her actions or with her management. He is not content to limit his critical eye and his aggressive competitiveness to his business world. At every occasion he must challenge his wife in all those areas which should belong to a woman and a homemaker. Jack carries his self-image of success in business over to his marriage. Since he has been so successful in business, it is surely not his failure in the marriage, so he blames his wife. The competitiveness and the aggressiveness that Jack inflicts upon his wife make her resentful, angry, and leave her many times with a feeling of "What's the use anyway? Whatever I do will be criticized, and he will tell me how much better he can do it." Instead of getting what he would like to see in his home, Jack reaps the whirlwind of his criticism by a withdrawn and sarcastic woman. Jack and Nancy with the help of their counselor must learn how to better fit and mesh with one another. Jack will have to acquire the insight that marriage cannot be run on the same basis as a business. Love and appreciation will have to be substituted for competitiveness and criticism. It is not easy to change ingrained attitudes and to play different roles at one time in business and at another time at home. Yet it can be done, and many couples have been helped through counseling and talking the matter through thoroughly.

OTHER HAZARDS TO THE MARITAL RELATIONSHIPS

In none of these cases discussed above did any of the individuals turn to an extramarital affair, to drinking, or to drugs to escape intolerable and aggravating situations. These individuals just happened to find their escape or support by other means. Many people who according to the psychiatrist have a proneness or are predisposed psychologically will find their escape from an intolerable marriage situation through an affair with another woman or man, by drowning their troubles in alcohol, or in extreme cases by becoming drug addicts.

The causes and the reasoning which drive one married man to become unfaithful to his wife, while another man who seems to suffer similar abuses in his marriage remains faithful, are most difficult to analyze or categorize. There is, of course, always the rationalization and the presently tolerated argument of "falling out of love" with one's wife and "falling madly in love" with this particular woman. In an age which has dramatized the importance of love and romance, such a stand is often projected, with little guilt or remorse, as a conscious, deliberate and justifiable action.

The marriage counselor who has worked with people who have had long-standing extramarital affairs, and still want to keep their marriage going, will testify to the fact that there are many irrational, distorted and unconscious causes for such human action. For many it does not bring happiness and relief, but torment and imprisonment. Dr. Leon Saul states: "The turning of a man away from his own wife and children to another woman is seen at all ages. Sometimes . . . it strikes like lightning. With others it is a slow, creeping, insidious and almost imperceptible slipping into an emotional quicksand. The analogy is apt, for many husbands resist this slow sinking; often they fight against it, and once engulfed, they feel not happiness but torment, not release from the bonds of marriage and convention, but an entrapment from which they cannot escape, from which they cannot any longer will to free themselves."

It is no easy matter to help such people find the way out of their sexual dilemma and out of their unconscious conflicts. Such situations and problems are beyond the depth of the average clergyman who has not had formal training in counseling or psychotherapy. Since there are many direct moral issues which conflict

with the stance of religion, it would be better that the clergyman
not involve himself in such a counselor-counselee relationship.
The clergyman could be of service to the individual in a referral
capacity. The individual should be referred to a psychiatrist if he
really wants to help himself. It is important that the mate of the
individual seeking help on such a problem also seek some counseling help for support and direction during this difficult period.
A clergyman trained in counseling could be of great service to
the family in such an instance.

SMOLDERING INFIDELITY

Barney and Mae have been married for thirty years. Their two
sons are married to two lovely women and a fine relationship
exists between the children and their parents. The children are
totally unaware of any conflict. Barney is a construction engineer
and owns and operates a large and well-known company which
has been erecting some of the largest skyscrapers in recent years.
Barney is very happy in his work and gains great satisfaction
from his achievement. He has always been generous in monies to
his wife and has been a good father to his sons. In the early
years of marriage there were some conflicts and difficulties which
were left to smolder and never explored or brought to the surface.
Barney sought comfort in an affair with another woman, who
worked in the office of the construction company. In counseling
it was revealed that Barney has carried on with this woman, some
fifteen years younger than he, for more than twenty years. Due
to the threats of his wife, he has broken off seeing her from time to
time, but has never been able, or never has wanted to extricate
himself from this triangle. He has great ambivalent feelings about
his relationship, both to his wife and to his lady friend. He seems
to want both, and if he could have his way, he would like to have
the situation remain unchanged. Now, after all these years, Mae

insists that he either make the break or she will sue for divorce. A year of intensive marriage counseling, in which both Barney and Mae have participated with great cooperation, has not resolved the problem. Mae has made tremendous efforts to improve her relationship with Barney, and he does not deny the fact. On the other hand, Barney is still indecisive and ambivalent about the choice, though he knows he must make one. Recently, Barney has accepted the suggestion to explore his problem in greater depth with a psychiatrist.

The problem of alcoholics in the United States has been steadily increasing since the war. Just as those who seek extramarital affairs for solutions to their problems, so do alcoholics use drink. Neither help themselves to overcome their basic problems. Instead, they cause great concern and anguish to their loved ones, and place the stability of the marriage and the family structure in great jeopardy. This pertains particularly to the alcoholic who, when under the effects of alcohol, cannot control his behavior, actions, or feelings. This has a direct bearing on work, earning, relations to spouse and to children. Today, alcoholism is no longer placed in the category of "moral choice," but is looked upon as a sickness. It is a disease which needs the attention of the doctor, the experienced counselor, or individuals like members of Alcoholics Anonymous, who have had considerable success in helping alcoholics.

RELIGIOUS COUNSELING

Counseling and helping people with their problems is a very ancient trade. In the biblical and rabbinic writings we discover references and connotations that the wise men of old served as counselors and advisers. Throughout the centuries men and women have turned to rabbis, priests, and ministers for counsel and directions, as well as for solace and strength in hours of distress. Today, more than ever before, people are turning to their religious leaders for help with problems, ranging from primary behavior disorders of their children to severe marital breakdowns. More and more clergymen are receiving training and experience in counseling and pastoral counseling, either through study at their particular seminary or at a pastoral clinical training center. They are prepared to counsel their parishioners or to help by referring them to other counselors, psychiatrists, or therapists as the cases may warrant.

Many clergymen are prepared to give their time and effort to help their congregants work through a crisis in a marriage or help a couple face boldly a difficulty that has arisen in their relationship. A clergyman who has had some training in counseling and has insight into dynamic psychology will be in a very good position to help married people with their marriage. He is not only a friend of the family, but he usually knows the people and even has easy access to the home. If he has served the congregation for any length of time, he usually has the confidence of his people and a good rapport with them, even before he starts to counsel with them. This in itself will be of great help in exploring the situation and getting down to the basics of the problems. If the marriage difficulty is not too involved and the personalities not neurotic in their behavior to each other, the clergyman may be able to help them. After all, marriage is a "holy matter" and "a blessing of God" which is the concern of the religious teacher. He will want to do everything in his command to help his people continue to see their marriage as a blessing and as "holiness" (Kedushin which means holiness is the Hebrew term used to designate marriage). The clergyman who is a trained counselor will so arrange his schedule as to enable him to do extensive marriage counseling with his parishioners. Yet, even in such a setting, the trained clergyman-marriage counselor should not get himself involved in very difficult or pathological marriage counseling cases. Such relationships are fraught with danger both for the minister and his congregants.

THE PREMARITAL INTERVIEW

More than in any other area of the "helping-people art" the clergyman is in an ideal position to work with couples to take constructive steps at the beginning of the marriage. Couples do come to clergymen to be married, and they can utilize this opportunity to do an important task in the education for marriage. Two or three hours spent with a couple in a premarital counseling interview can do more than ten hours of marriage counseling after the conflicts and hostilities have seared the victims and done the damage.

The premarital interview not only gives the clergyman the opportunity for the development of a rapport and relationship which can be invaluable in later years, but can help young people to experience the value of counseling and the help that results from just talking it through. In such a counseling session there will be the opportunity to explore love and sex, money and budgets, in-laws and family relations, and the place of religion and the church or the synagogue in a marriage. The couple will also learn for the first time in such a session that marital problems are fairly routine. They will hear that people do not find instantaneous adjustment and happiness in marriage, and that there are people who understand this very well.

Also, the premarital interview will help the young people to realize that it is perfectly all right to seek professional help—as one would seek other kinds of professional help when in need. This is basic to the whole dilemma of whether or not to seek help when marital problems arise. People tend to put off seeking help, sometimes because they feel ashamed or afraid or just reluctant to do something as strange as talking to an outsider about intimate affairs. Many times they wait too long after the problem has arisen, and then it is ever so difficult for the couple to find their way back to love and a wholesome marital relationship. Ministers can do much in their teaching and preaching to bring home the importance of talking things through, of the primacy of communication and the first aids of counseling in marriage.

EDUCATION FOR MARRIAGE

Ministers can begin even earlier than at the time of the premarital interview to help inculcate the needed wholesome attitudes for making marriage a workable and cooperative venture. Through his sermons, religious school curriculum and adult education, he can profoundly impress upon his congregants the sanctity of marriage. There is another force in the synagogue and church tradition which leaders and teachers have not utilized to its fullest potential. Each religious tradition has developed disciplines and guidelines which can be of invaluable help in directing and motivating individuals into wholesome relationships and positive thinking. Commitments which call for a life of concern and consideration for others and require disciplined patterns of action can greatly influence what we do and what we say. Religious commitments in all faiths make for a more meaningful life when they are fulfilled with understanding and sincerity. Fulfillment of religious commitments help to convey a sense of holiness to the smallest of human acts.

Education for marriage, with a sense of commitment to make it holy, does not begin in the public school, the church, the synagogue, the religious school, or the Sunday school. These institutions are only supplementary forces in the development of healthy and sane attitudes about marriage and family life. Education for marriage begins in the home, and learning the art of love, giving, cooperating, and the sense of responsibility must start from the cradle and continue through the formative years of childhood and adolescence. Courses in family life education, the educative or the psychological processes in premarital or marriage counseling cannot shape people into loving and giving personalities. Counseling can only help people to understand some of their limitations as well as to appreciate and utilize their strengths and thus help them to fit and mesh better in their relationships with others. Only the home and loving parents can shape children into people who love and share graciously. Parents, with the support of their church or synagogue, can profoundly impress their children with the sanctity of marriage and help them affirm "our belief that God is an active partner in sustaining and enriching the husband-wife relationship in marriage."

22

The End of a Marriage

•

JAMES EMERSON

James Emerson is Director of the Community Service Society
of New York City. Trained as a minister with a doctorate in pastoral care, he served Presbyterian Churches in Pennsylvania, Illinois,
New Jersey, and Long Island and Westchester Counties, New York,
before deciding to become a missionary to the urban ghetto. His deep
concern for people has been reflected in his preaching, teaching, and
writing, especially in his two books, *Divorce, the Church and Remarriage* and *The Dynamics of Forgiveness.*

•

WHAT AN IRONY! To conclude a book on marriage with its failure!
Or have the hippies really won the day? Is it true that the church
and synagogue really agree with them—marriage is fine when you
have a love-in, but can be easily dropped when you do not? Or is
it perhaps that there is a reality about marriage which must be
faced if marriage is to succeed?

There is a sense in which each statement may have a point. Especially for those who work repeatedly with marriage failures, there
come moments, if not days, of cynicism about a book such as
this. And although the new morality is rejected by many and the
hippy approach is loudly decried, the noise of these reactions almost says, "Methinks the lady doth protest too much." The fact
is that many talk one ethic but live another.

Yet, despite all of this, precisely those who work regularly with marriage failures are the ones who also continue to speak and write about the importance, the value, and the place of the family. What drives them on is the awareness of strengths and dividends and means of success that outweigh the effect of the disappointments.

There are two reasons for facing the "death of a marriage." The first is: Facing any death provides an opportunity to prepare for it. This preparation may succeed in avoiding death for a while—as in preventive medicine. When the marriage death does come, this preparation will help the couple meet it without being completely destroyed by the experience.

The other reason is the freedom that can come in being aware of death. It is my conviction that marriage does not succeed on the basis of coercion, but on the basis of inner freedom. Whenever two people enter into any kind of relationship, that freedom is partly surrendered. The very awareness that a marriage can die places upon the couple the constant freedom of a choice. "Do I want to keep this marriage alive or not?" That freedom in itself is an unrecognized but basic part of a marriage foundation. Consider this example:

Not long ago I counseled a man who had reached what I call "the summit" of adult experience. The summit is that point where a person is not yet ready for retirement, but he has gone as high (in terms of prestige) as he is going. He still has some good years, but he is not apt to change jobs again or gain another promotion.

A person in such a situation often feels trapped. Life is passing him. He does not mind becoming a grandfather, but he suddenly realizes he is married to a grandmother—and that bothers him. He may, as did this man, question his faith and the purpose of his living.

In the course of this mood, this man went to a conference where he met a most attractive woman who was just a few years younger than he. The relationship that developed was important and real. Call it "love." In that relationship, the man in question suddenly realized that he could marry someone other than his wife. In terms of another person, he had an option—not because she or he wanted to get married, but because he could be attractive to other people. With this awareness, he realized that his marriage could die, and that he had to make a choice. He had to decide the priority he would give his marriage in his life. Out of this very freedom he was able to say, "I now have no question. My first priority is to have my marriage work." And it did.

The one place where the main-line Jewish, Catholic, Orthodox and Protestant groups agree is that a marriage ends with death.

Before we look at the question as to the ways in which a marriage can die, there is a fundamental lesson to be learned from this fact of life. The lesson is the danger of making a god out of one's husband or wife.

The romantic literature of today carries an adulation of the one who is loved. In recent generations, such phrases as "adore you" or "worship you" were frequently heard. Today, the sense of hanging on or finding one's total security in another person is suggested in a song by the Beatles, "I wanna hold your hand," or in their hit: "Will you love me, will you need me when I'm sixty-four?"

Most people would quickly assert that they do not make a god out of other people. Certainly, most of us do not think that we do; yet most of us greatly underestimate the amount of emotional investment we have in the person we marry. That investment is there even when a couple fights. Consider the feelings of children toward parents who are not only too strict, but almost brutal. I am constantly amazed at the way in which children who are terribly unhappy over the treatment of parents become even more shaken when that parent is suddenly removed. There is a point where a child may run away or rebel; but let the parent be the one to leave, and note the reaction. There is an emotional investment even in one who is hated.

If this is true with children who had no choice in selecting a parent, how much more is it true in a husband and wife. Out of a free act, shared triumphs and tragedies deepen the romantic love that first attracted them. The stars of the first kiss may pass but the deep emotional investment of one person in the other grows. In some individuals, this emotional investment can grow too much!

I recall a man whose wife died. He wept at the funeral, as would be expected. Several years later, he still wept whenever something reminded him of his wife. Even that is not unusual. After ten years, however, his grieving for his wife was so great that he could not meet people socially. His emotional investment in her had literally made her a goddess. When she had gone from his world, he could not function.

By contrast, another man was the victim of a tragic fire not long after he and his bride returned from their honeymoon. They were at a nightclub together when a fire broke out. Both were injured; his wife died of the injuries. The man had understandable feelings of grief and guilt: grief for her death; guilt for having taken her to the nightclub. In the course of time, he took a trip in which he revisited every place he had ever taken his wife. In the course of the pilgrimage, he was able to come to terms with her death. His feeling for her was genuine; but he did not make a goddess either of her or of his feelings.

Two people who marry need to find something that transcends both of them in which they put their ultimate emotional investment. Faith in God frees one from the danger of making a god out of the other person (it is hard to live up to being a god); it gives a basis for the marriage to succeed.

OTHER DEATHS OF MARRIAGE

Can marriage die other than by the physical death of a partner? In a qualified sense, all groups accept the view that a marriage can die in other ways. For both Protestant and Jew, the death of a marriage is recognized through the act of divorce. For the Roman Catholic and some Orthodox, the death is recognized by annulment.

In a technical sense, the Roman Catholic would not consider the annulment as the death of a marriage. For him, marriage is a sacrament. A sacrament cannot die. The question is whether or not it was there in the first place. Annulment is a way of saying that it was never there.

From a practical standpoint, however, annulment carries with it all that others consider to be the death of a marriage. If two people marry contrary to the laws of the church, live together for a considerable period, and then separate with an annulment, a relationship has died. Just because a relationship may have been sinful does not mean it has not been real.

With that qualification, then, it can be said that all religious groups see that a marriage can die without a husband or wife being dead; but they disagree on the means of this death.

In the Roman Catholic Church, divorce is not recognized. For economic reasons civil divorce is permitted to those who separate. But even then Catholics are not free to marry. However, Father Victor J. Pospishil, in a book entitled *Divorce and Remarriage* (Herder and Herder, 1967), makes a surprisingly good case for recognizing divorce within the Roman tradition. This professor from Manhattan College uses both biblical and patristic literature to argue that although man cannot put two asunder, God can. This position is hardly official, but it is evidence that the position of Rome may indeed be open to more discussion in the future.

At the opposite extreme from the Catholic Church is the Hebrew position. For the Jewish people, marriage is both a civil and religious act, and so is divorce. A Jewish couple who wish to be divorced must obtain a religious divorce document as well as a civil one.

The mood behind the Jewish view accentuates the difference from Christian groups. There is a long and interesting history of

Jewish divorce law. There have been conservative groups (the Shammai school) and liberal groups (the Hillel school). Yet, basic is a quote from the Talmud which reads, "It is better for four people to be happy than for two to be miserable."

Whereas the general Christian mood in the last centuries was to see remarriage as something allowed rather grudgingly, the Jewish view did not frown on remarriage. In fact, it saw the purpose of divorce as that of putting the person involved in a position to get married and thus stabilize his life.

With regard to the Protestants, one cannot speak of "a Protestant position on divorce." Regardless of denomination, there are fundamentalist groups that will allow divorce only for adultery. There are other groups that seemingly have little or no restrictions. In general, however, two principles will be found in various denominations.

First is the principle that the couple is part of something bigger than themselves. Thus, the Episcopal Church requires that a couple contemplating divorce must go to a priest to have the matter discussed. In the event of a desired remarriage after a divorce or annulment, the matter must be reviewed by the bishop and by a group designated by the bishop. In most other churches, the minister himself makes the ultimate decisions, but the laws lay great stress on the responsibility of the whole church for the couple in question.

Second is the principle of concern for the individuals themselves. In the Lutheran Church, for example, there is no basic law. However, there is set up an excellent statement under the Board of Social Ministry which guides both ministers and parishioners in matters that relate to all aspects of marriage. The Presbyterian Church in the United States (Southern) has the finest approach, in my view, because it has established opportunities for counsel and guidance at local levels throughout the denomination. The rules it has given relate to a process that can help a person rather than to regulations that box him in.

What can a couple learn about marriage from this divergent view of the churches? A couple can sense that for the one who believes in God, more is involved in marriage than just themselves. In one sense, this means a responsibility. As the statement from Vatican II put it, marriage has a bearing on all humanity. The well-being of society is based on the well-being of the family. In another sense, awareness that the two are not the only ones involved in a marriage brings a great hope. It means that when tension and difficulty come, they are not alone. There is a group that surrounds them with compassion and concern. They have a place to turn.

WHAT KILLS A MARRIAGE?

At the outset, we observed that awareness of the possible death of a marriage can help us develop that which will prevent the death. What then does kill a marriage? What are the dangers against which we must guard?

Historically, religious groups have identified two human acts that killed a marriage. One was adultery, the other desertion.

Historically, religious groups have seen marriage as either killed before it was born or destroyed after it had been started. Lack of virginity, inability or unwillingness to engage in sexual relations, or some hidden malady have usually been recognized as grounds for declaring a marriage null. Adultery and desertion, for all except Roman Catholics, have been considered grounds for divorce.

From modern studies of family life, however, I would identify the following as killers of marriage:

1) *Failure to leave one's parents.* In more instances than people realize, an emotional bondage to parents interferes with a marriage and ultimately kills it. The bondage may be as obvious as inability to leave home at all. The bondage may be a deep attachment where, as in one instance, the girl wakes up night after night calling for her father. The bondage may be subtle. It may

be a boy who has never adequately dealt with anger toward his parents. It may be a man who, unknowingly, projects mother images on his wife and thus reacts to her more as a mother than a wife. Whatever the form of expression, a person cannot become one flesh with a spouse without ceasing to be one flesh with parents.

2) *Failure to be honest about one's feelings.* Shakespeare's Polonius said to his son, "To thine own self be true . . . and thou canst not then be false to any man." The inability to be honest with oneself about the feelings one has leads to two problems. The ability to be honest about one's feelings is important because no one can deal with something unless he knows what that something is. Unless one is honest with oneself, he will be false to others, and that falseness destroys a marriage.

3) *Failure to deal with one's feelings, once known.* Unfortunately, many think that psychology teaches only the need for self-expression. If a youngster is a brat, the modern mother is pictured as saying, "Oh, he's just expressing himself." Many girls have been told by men that they should agree to "go to bed" because "I feel the need for sex." Actually, there is a great difference between having a feeling and deciding how to act with regard to one's feeling. The real value of therapy is not that it frees a person to do what he feels like doing, but that it enables a person to learn how to deal with his feelings so that he is free to act in spite of them. Freud called it sublimation.

4) *Too readily resorting to divorce.* Divorce can be seen as a recognition that a marriage has died. In such an instance, it is simply a means of recognizing something that has happened. Divorce, however, can also be used as matter of convenience. The Hollywood divorce is typically a divorce used to kill a marriage.

Although various religions do not agree on the basis for recognizing the death of a marriage, or even on the list of things that can be said to kill a marriage, they do agree on what is necessary to prevent that death: commitment.

Without firm resolve it is hard to imagine the survival of any marriage, for anything that leads to the death of marriage can be overcome only with pain. Whether it is a small bird being shoved out of the security of a nest or a grown man or woman leaving home, it is not easy to leave the family. That can cause great personal pain. Honesty about one's feelings may seem easy, but it is not. In a country that is conditioned to think of marriage as "living happily ever after," experience of real anger at one's wife will usually be accompanied by experience of guilt. Awareness of being in love with another person may often bring with it a sense of fear. Only dedication to one's marriage as a first priority will result in having the guts to endure the pain, the guilt, the fear, and work through the problem. When a marriage is in difficulty, one will insist on what the other must do. When there is determination, a person is able to ask, "What must I do?"

WHAT CAN BE DONE

Some marriages will fail. Yet that sad fact must not blind us to the greater truth that something can be done.

The answer comes when forgiveness is realized as a personal experience. The individual who has come to terms with life so that he experiences forgiveness is himself able to forgive. This ability does not solve all problems, but gives a freedom to deal creatively with all problems. That is why the person who has any degree of faith in God will have an enormous advantage. Belief in God will not solve the problem or reduce the struggle. However, faith brings the conviction that somewhere there is a meaning for one's life, that somewhere there is a "purpose for me," that somehow one is forgiven, "regardless." That conviction is a lifeline that allows one to survive the struggle and the pain of dealing with the killers of a marriage.

The need to experience forgiveness is also the reason for turning to counselors. The person who is not too proud to ask for help has a great chance for success, because a good counselor helps convey the reality of forgiveness. Not all counselors or therapists have adequate training or are equally good. Yet two committed people, willing to endure the struggle under the guidance of a good therapist who accepts them as they are, will emerge with the discovery of inner resources and spiritual strength they never believed possible.

In my personal view, then, above all else, the fact that a marriage can die demands the gift of forgiveness. Whether one begins with the atonement in Yom Kippur or the prayer of Jesus expressed from the cross, all faiths begin with forgiveness and place forgiveness at the heart of family life.

A Final Word and a Prayer

•

THE EDITORS AND CONTRIBUTORS to this book join in saying to you: Have confidence in yourself, your partner, and your marriage! For all marriages are a venture in faith—the faith that you and your spouse can make your marriage a joyous fulfillment provided there is care and concern, compassion and growing understanding of one another. Your firm commitment can carry you through rough seas and destructive storms. With wholesome behavior, attitudes, and activities, your marriage can bear the label: "Made in Heaven."

ETERNAL FATHER, enable us to have faith in our marriage and make our home a place wherein Your divine presence is felt. Make our home a sanctuary wherein the light of love, peace, contentment, and compassionate understanding are found in abundance—where we worship You through kindness and concern for one another.

May Your law be our guide at all times so that we distinguish between good and evil, right and wrong, justice and injustice, the important and the trivial. Help us joyfully fulfill all our responsibilities to one another, to our fellowman, and to You. May we be patient and forebearing in the face of trials and persistent in the face of difficulties.

Teach us to live each day wisely and well as we share life's journey.

Amen.

Recommended Reading

•

Ayrault, Evelyn W., *You Can Raise Your Handicapped Child*. New York: G. P. Putnam's Sons, 1964.

Barbeau, Clayton C., *The Head of the Family*. Chicago: Henry Regnery Co., 1961.

Bird, Joseph and Lois, *The Freedom of Sexual Love*. New York: Doubleday and Co., Inc., 1967.

Caffarel, Henri, *Love and Grace in Marriage*. Notre Dame: Fides, 1960.

Capon, Robert Farrar, *Bed and Board*. New York: Simon and Schuster, 1965.

Cervantes, Lucius F., *And God Made and Woman*. Chicago: Henry Regnery Co., 1959.

Clemens, Alphonse H., *Design for Successful Marriage*. Englewood Cliffs, N.J., 1964.

Clinebell, H. J., Jr., *Mental Health Through Christian Community*. Nashville: Abingdon Press, 1965.

Dominian, Jacob, *Christian Marriage: the Challenge of Change*. Chicago: Franciscan Herald Press, 1967.

Evoy, John J., and Maureen O'Keefe, *The Man and The Woman*. New York: Sheed and Ward, 1968.

Folkman, Jerome D., *The Cup of Life*. New York: The Jonathan David Co., 1955.

Folkman, Jerome D., *Design for Jewish Living*. New York: Union of American Hebrew Congregations, 1965.

Gittelsohn, Roland B., *My Beloved Is Mine—Judaism and Marriage*. New York: Union of American Hebrew Congregations, 1969.

Golden, Janet, *The Quite Possible She*. New York: Herder and Herder, 1966. Paperback: St. Meinrad, Ind.: Abbey Press, 1967.

Goodman, Philip and Henna, *The Jewish Marriage Anthology*. Philadelphia: Jewish Publ. Soc. of America, 1965.

Gordis, Robert, *Sex and the Family in the Jewish Tradition*. New York: Burning Bush Press, 1967.

Gosling, J. C. B., *Marriage and the Love of God*. St. Meinrad, Ind.: Abbey Press, 1968.

Haas, Harold, *Marriage*. Philadelphia: Fortress Press, 1960.

Haring, Bernard, *Marriage in the Modern World*. Westminster, Md.: Newman Press, 1965.

Harrington, Janette T., and Muriel S. Webb, *Who Cares?* New York: Friendship Press, 1962.

Haughton, Rosemary, *Problems of Christian Marriage*. New York: Paulist Press, 1968.

Haughton, Rosemary, *Holiness of Sex*. St. Meinrad, Ind.: Abbey Press, 1969.

Hoyde, Howard, *The Neo-Married*. Valley Forge, Pa.: Judson Press, 1968.

In Holy Matrimony. (Committee authored.) Nashville: Methodist Publishing House, 1958.

Kelly, George H., *The Catholic Family Handbook*. New York: Random House, 1959.

Kephart, William M., *The Family, Society, and the Individual*. Boston: Houghton Mifflin, Co., 1966.

Lundberg, Ferdinand, and Farnham, Marynia F., *Modern Woman, The Lost Sex*. New York: Harper and Brothers, 1959.

Mace, David R., *Whom God Hath Joined*. Philadelphia: Westminster Press, 1953.

Magoun, F. A., *Love and Marriage*. New York: Harper and Brothers, 1956.

Max, Morris, and Chavel, Charles D., *Marriage at Home—A Jewish Guide for Marital Happiness*. New York: Rabbinical Council of America, 1959.

Mental Retardation: A Family Crisis. (Group authored.) New York: Group for the Advancement of Psychiatry, 1963.

Mudd, Emily, and Aron Krich, eds., *Man and Wife*. New York: Norton & Co., 1957.

Novak, Michael, ed., *The Experience of Marriage: The Testimony of Catholic Laymen*. New York: Macmillan, 1965.

Oraison, Marc, *Man and Wife*. New York: Macmillan, 1965.

Palmer, Charles E., *Religion and Rehabilitation*. Springfield, Ill.: Charles C. Thomas, 1968.

Planque, Daniel, *The Christian Couple*. Notre Dame: Fides, 1963.

Robinson, Marie, *The Power of Sexual Surrender*. New York: New American Library Signet Book, 1959.

Rodenmayer, Robert, *I, John, Take Thee, Mary*. New York: Seabury Press, 1962.

Saul, Leon J., M.D., *Fidelity and Infidelity, And What Makes or Breaks a Marriage*. Philadelphia: J. B. Lippincott Co., 1967.

Schillebeeckx, Edw. C., *Marriage: Human Reality and Saving Mystery*. New York: Sheed and Ward, 1966.

Schnepp, Gerald J., *To God Through Marriage*. Milwaukee: Bruce Publ. Co., 1967.

Sex, Family, and Society: The Theological Focus. (Committee authored.) New York: Association Press, 1966.

Sweazey, George, *In Holy Marriage*. New York: Harper & Row, 1966.

Tansey, Anne, *Where To Get Help for Your Family*. St. Meinrad, Ind.: Abbey Press, 1967.

Thomas, John L., *The Catholic Viewpoint on Marriage and the Family*. Garden City, N.Y.: Hanover House, 1958.

Tournier, Paul, *The Meaning of Persons*. New York: Harper and Brothers, 1957.

Trese, Leo J., *Parent and Child*. St. Meinrad, Ind.: Abbey Press, 1968.

Trevett, Reginald, *Sex and Personal Growth*. St. Meinrad, Ind.: Abbey Press, 1967.

Watkin, Aelred, *The Enemies of Love*. New York: P. J. Kenedy and Sons, 1958.

Werner, Bishop Hazen, *Christian Family Living*. Nashville: The Graded Press, 1958.

Weyergans, Franz, *An Adventure in Love*. St. Meinrad, Ind.: Abbey Press, 1967.

Winter, Gibson, *Love and Conflict*. New York: Doubleday and Co., Inc., 1961.